AS GOD MADE THEM

DANIEL WEBSTER AT MARSHFIELD

AS GOD MADE THEM

Portraits of Some
Nineteenth-Century Americans

BY

GAMALIEL BRADFORD

KENNIKAT PRESS/PORT WASHINGTON, N. Y.

AS GOD MADE THEM

Copyright 1929 by Gamaliel Bradford
Reissued in 1969 by Kennikat Press by arrangement with
Houghton Mifflin Company
Library of Congress Catalog Card No: 74-85992
SBN 8046-0540-8

Manufactured by Taylor Publishing Company   Dallas, Texas

ESSAY AND GENERAL LITERATURE INDEX REPRINT SERIES

PREFACE

THE portrait of Horace Greeley contained in this book was written four years ago. Since that time Mr. Don C. Seitz has written his brilliant and scholarly study of Greeley. Mr. Seitz has hunted out much original material and has developed various aspects of Greeley's career and character much more fully than I had space to do. But it seems to me that the fundamental lines of that striking and picturesque personality, as established in my portrait, are not materially modified in the later biography.

I take occasion to express my indebtedness in my study of Edwin Booth to the admirable theatrical collection gathered by Mr. Robert Gould Shaw and deposited by him in the Harvard College Library. This collection is invaluable to students of the American drama and the courteous coöperation of Mr. Shaw and Mrs. Hall greatly increases the usefulness of it. I am also indebted to the officials of the Boston Public Library, and above all to the staff of the Boston Athenæum, without whose constant and efficient assistance my work could not be done at all.

GAMALIEL BRADFORD

Wellesley Hills, Mass.

CONTENTS

ILLUSTRATIONS

AS GOD MADE THEM

I
DANIEL WEBSTER

CHRONOLOGY

DANIEL WEBSTER

Born, Salisbury, New Hampshire, January 18, 1782.
Graduated, Dartmouth, 1801.
Admitted to Bar, Boston, 1805.
Married Grace Fletcher, June 24, 1808.
In House of Representatives, 1813–1817.
Plymouth Oration delivered, 1820.
In House of Representatives, 1823–1827.
Entered Senate, 1828.
Married Caroline LeRoy, December 18, 1829.
Reply to Hayne, 1830.
Visit to England, 1839.
Secretary of State, 1841–1843.
Again in Senate, 1845.
Secretary of State, 1850–1852.
Died, Marshfield, October 24, 1852.

DANIEL WEBSTER'S DESK AND DISPATCH-BOX

These articles used by Webster, together with a collection of manuscript letters, some unpublished, are now in the possession of the author,
whose grandfather, Henry W. Kinsman, was Webster's partner.

AS GOD MADE THEM

DANIEL WEBSTER

I

HOMER tells us that Odysseus was insignificant in appearance. His stature was low, his features were common, his bearing was awkward. It was only when he spoke that men were carried away by the swift, enchanting magic of his words. The case was quite different with Webster. When he walked through the streets, strangers paused to look at him, and his mere aspect seized and dominated before he spoke at all. He was a solidly built man, seeming larger than he actually was, and splendidly dignified in his largeness. His shoulders were broad, his chest was massive, his head was poised with an Olympian grandeur. He was very dark — dark hair, dark skin, dark eyes. His rugged features could and not infrequently did express genial kindness and even sympathetic tenderness. But when he wished to control, to conquer, to overcome, the stern intensity of his look was almost irresistible. Special stress is laid upon his eyes. They were deep-

3

set under craggy brows. The whites were unusually white and large, and this enhanced the blazing ardor of the dark iris and pupil, which seemed to fix and penetrate with a searching glare that struck right down to the heart of friend and enemy alike. Altogether, there have been few orators whose outward aspect so magnificently anticipated and reenforced their power of speech.

Webster was born in Salisbury, New Hampshire, in 1782. His parents were rugged, thrifty farming people, who gave their children everything they could, and especially education. As a boy, Daniel was not strong and preferred books to farm work, though he lived much out of doors and always loved the fields and woods. He got the public school teaching of his time, then went to Phillips Academy, Exeter, and to Dartmouth College, and later studied law as it was studied in lawyers' offices in those days. He settled and practiced first in Portsmouth, then in Boston, and soon made himself prominent and successful. But he had a natural drift toward politics, from the day when he read the Constitution as printed on a cotton handkerchief. He entered Congress, first as a strong Federal, opposed to the Madison administration and the War of 1812, and heartily in favor of free trade,

a position which he gave up later, with much sub-
sequent reproach. In 1830 he established his great
reputation by his Senate speeches against Hayne in
behalf of the Union. He supported Jackson against
the Nullifiers of the Constitution, but opposed him
in the matter of the Bank. In 1842 he negotiated
the Ashburton Treaty with England, as Secretary
of State under Tyler. All through his earlier career
he proclaimed his opposition to slavery, but in 1850
he supported Clay's Compromise, believing that it
was needed to save the Union, and by his arguments for the Fugitive Slave Law he made himself
obnoxious to the Abolitionists, who asserted that
he had sacrificed his conscience in the hope of getting the presidency. He died in the autumn of
1852. Webster was twice married and had three
sons and two daughters. Only one son survived
him.

It will be well to begin by analyzing some of the
most marked elements in Webster's professional
and political life. In the first place, it is clear that
he had an enormous power of work. Senator Lodge,
whose 'Life of Webster,' though written in the
eighties under the influence of the Abolitionist
tradition, gives perhaps the most acute study of his
character, insists that he was naturally indolent.

In a sense this is true enough. Webster had one of those large, rich, self-indulgent natures, which work only when there is an incentive, not for the pure pleasure of it. Like Sir Walter Scott, with whom he is often compared, he would no doubt have said, 'Set me anything to do as a task and it is inconceivable the desire I have to do something else.' But, again like Scott, Webster had the power of working vastly when he chose, and above all he could concentrate and direct his work so that every atom of it told. If industry is measured by achievement, the charge of indolence becomes really laughable, and, once more like Scott, Webster was an early riser, and got a day's work out of the way before most men are ready to begin. The indolent are not apt to be acquainted with the first hours after a summer sunrise.

Something the same contradiction appears in another aspect of Webster's character, that of courage and independence. His whole physique suggested energy, determination, a royal disregard of the dictation of others. As he himself expressed it, in his Faneuil Hall Speech, in 1842, when he was attacked for not leaving Tyler's Cabinet with his colleagues: 'I am a little hard to coax, but as to being driven, that is out of the question.' [1] It

6

would have appeared so, if you looked at him. All his life he declared that he followed an independent course, and absolutely refused to let the chains of party be riveted upon him too closely. Yet, owing perhaps to the elements suggested above in connection with indolence, he sometimes allowed himself to be affected by considerations hardly compatible with being completely independent, and his peculiar financial circumstances, which will be more developed later, exposed him, as time went on, to charges of undue influence, which have always clouded his reputation to some extent. Again and again, as one studies him, one is reminded of the comment of Carlyle on Thackeray, 'a big man, not a strong man.' The distinction is somewhat too emphatic, when applied to Webster, but it has its significance.

On the other hand, the disposition to yield to others, or at any rate to learn from them, has its good side, and may be a source of power as well as of weakness. Webster is often accused of having what would now be called 'an ear to the ground,' of being too eagerly on the watch for what men were saying and wishing, and governing his conduct by it. He writes home to know what people think, what their judgment and opinion are. But surely no public man loses by this. The art of listening, especially in a great speaker, is of the utmost value, and Webster had it in perfection. He heard what others had to say, deferred to their judgment, and formed his own by it, and the use of intelligence in this fashion is in the highest degree profitable. I hardly know finer testimony to statesmanlike quality than President Tyler's account of Webster's attitude toward the other members of the Cabinet, who were all men of less standing than he and naturally inclined to look up to him: 'He was ready at all times to receive, to consider, and if proper, to adopt the suggestions of others. He went farther. He courted the severest criticism of his writings or opinions. . . . Every suggestion of addition or alteration was weighed by him with the same impartiality as if he had been the critic and the production criticized had been the work of another.' [2]

Again a curious contradiction in the elements of Webster's character appears in his larger practical dealings with men. He seems to have been generally cordial and friendly. His manner in earlier days is said to have been somewhat rough and repellent, but later this mellowed to a dignity which was always kindly and often sympathetic. He made it a rule not to say harsh things, either in private or in public, and tried to eliminate all such speech from his printed works. He had few enemies and few serious quarrels. John Randolph challenged him; but Randolph was ready to quarrel with anybody, and the letter in which Webster refuses to meet him is as free from false bravado as it is from fear. John Quincy Adams long bore him a grudge, as he did to so many, and even writes: 'Such is human nature, in the gigantic intellect, the envious temper, the ravenous ambition, and the rotten heart of Daniel Webster.' [3] But the general record is far more favorable and indicates that Webster was on good terms with most people and deserved to be. Especially, the testimony of his humbler neighbors near the farm at Marshfield, Massachusetts, which was so dear to him, goes to prove that he was kindly, considerate, and helpful. He had the invaluable quality of remembering not only men's faces and names, but the little details of their personal history. Yet, on the other hand, he had not the magnetic attraction which gives a leader an enthusiastic partisan following, and this lack of support kept him from attaining the object of his highest ambition, the presidency. When one compares him with such born leaders as Jefferson, Clay, Blaine, or Roosevelt, one sees what the difference in the public attitude was. Men respected Webster, they admired him, they quoted him, they imitated him; but they voted for somebody else, often for those whom they knew to be his inferiors.

Even the critical John Quincy Adams speaks of Webster's 'gigantic intellect,' and the analysis of this intellect is especially interesting. As regards early education, indiscreet biographers appear to exaggerate somewhat both the boy's aptitude and his industry, in their misguided zeal to make him appear in every respect a model. His father and mother and much beloved elder brother, Ezekiel, did all they could to furnish opportunity, and Daniel responded, if not always with persistence, at any rate with the fire and the insight of genius. He learned what interested him with extraordinary rapidity, and especially with his singular faculty for getting what he wanted when and where he wanted it.

His reading may not always have been very solid or systematic, but it was extensive and ranged in all sorts of fields. He read the great English writers, remembered them, and used them with astonishing aptness and efficacy for his purposes. As he himself vividly puts the advantages of such general reading: 'I have never learned anything which I wish to forget, except how badly some people have behaved; and I every day find, on almost every subject, that I wish I had more knowledge than I possess, seeing that I could produce it, if not for use, yet for effect.' [4]

Perhaps Webster's chief intellectual quality was his extreme shrewdness and penetrative power. Whether the question that came before him was a trial for murder, or a point of constitutional law, or a subtlety of political expedience, he went straight to the important issue, seized upon it, disentangled it, and presented it to those concerned, with compelling and convincing vigor. He was never at a loss, never disconcerted, never allowed his opponent to put him at a disadvantage, but on the contrary was quick to turn a difficult and what seemed a disastrous situation to his own benefit. In comparison with all the biographer's anecdotes about his virtuous youth, I much relish the story Lincoln picked up, which may or may not be true, but is infinitely characteristic. When Webster was a boy in the district school, he was not noted for tidiness. Finally the teacher, in despair, told him that if he appeared again with such dirty hands, she should thrash him. He did appear, in the same condition. 'Daniel,' she said, 'hold out your hand.'

Daniel spat on his palm, rubbed it on the seat of his trousers, and held it out. The teacher surveyed it in disgust. 'Daniel,' she said, 'if you can find me another hand in this school that is dirtier than that, I will let you off.' Daniel promptly held out the other hand, and she had to keep her word. That was Daniel Webster, in school, and in the Supreme Court, and the Senate of the United States. He always produced the other hand, when it was needed, and won his case.

As Webster's intelligence was clear and penetrating, so it was orderly, systematic, and cogent. He not only perceived points, he arranged them, so that their full bearing and effect were instantly and overwhelmingly appreciated. Yet, while his thinking was always direct and forcible, it does not seem to me that he was inclined to general speculation, or very skillful in it. Emerson, whose own tendency was so different, expresses this almost too strongly: 'Hence a sterility of thought, the want of generalizing in his speeches, and the curious fact that, with a general ability which impresses all the world, there is not a single general remark, not an observation on life and manners, not an aphorism that can pass into literature from his writings.' 5 And this sterility as regards general philosophical matters affects even Webster's political thinking. His speeches analyze and elucidate special questions and received principles with admirable effect, but he rarely raises or suggests broad political speculation such as is so common in Burke.* And there is the further point, that this absence of speculative analysis in general extends most markedly to the analysis of the man's soul. We have hundreds of Webster's letters, but I have found them pitifully barren, rammed full of superficial fact, but empty of revealing touches. He himself suggests that he did not dare to write freely, for fear of getting into print, but the barrenness applies as much to his youth, when there can have been no such fear, as to his age. Compared with the great masters of the letter-writing art, he reveals so little that one sometimes wonders, very unjustly, whether there was much to reveal. But there are plenty of other great figures in the world, as to whom the same query might be raised on the same ground.

In other words, we have in Webster, either by nature or by habit, or by both, the distinctly legal

* On this subject of Webster's political thinking it is well to read the excellent chapter in *The Romantic Revival in America*, in which Professor Parrington analyzes the three stages of Webster's development, first as a sound if conservative political thinker, then as a lawyer, and finally as a politician.

13

type of mind, and it yet remains for some one to make an analytical study of the profoundly important part played by the lawyer in the growth and movement of American politics. The lawyer tends to take things as they are, and to maintain and defend them as they are. He is nurtured and firmly disciplined in the respect for tradition and precedent. As Burke says of one brilliant specimen: 'He was bred to the law, which is, in my opinion, one of the first and noblest of human sciences; a science which does more to quicken and invigorate the understanding than all the other kinds of learning put together; but it is not apt, except in persons very happily born, to open and liberalize the mind in the same proportion.' [6] In his earlier years Webster expressed some doubt as to his profession in various aspects. Its morality, he says, 'is a matter of doubt, or rather it is a matter of no doubt at all.' [7] But as time went on, the legal habit became pretty thoroughly ingrained. He had extraordinary quickness and ingenuity of reasoning; but this was not so much devoted to the analysis of fundamental theory as to the interpretation of principles already accepted and established. In politics, the American Constitution was the highest type of political wisdom. It was not necessary to go behind it or beyond it. And the great function of Daniel Webster's mind and of Daniel Webster's tongue was to make the Constitution clear, applicable, and enduring.

In a sense, of the tongue above all; for it is undeniable that it was Webster's power of speech that made his greatness, and it is interesting to reflect what he might have been without it. With his physique, with his intellectual grasp and vigor, no doubt he would have made a mark in the world, even if he had been tongue-tied. But his supreme prominence, his extensive influence over men, were necessarily bound up with his gift of oratory. Those who are more competent to make the comparison than I am insist that he belongs with the great orators of the world. I am unable to read Demosthenes in the original with the facility which would be essential to forming a judgment; but when I turn to Cicero or to Burke, I confess that I seem to find something that I do not find in Webster. It must always be remembered, however, that in oratory as printed we do not have what was originally spoken, or very rarely. Few studies of style can be more instructive than the comparison of one of Webster's most brilliant paragraphs, the conclusion of the 'Reply to Hayne,' as finally printed and as taken down warm from his lips by the stenographer. The final form is more resonant, more elaborately literary; but I find the original more impressive in its simplicity and genuineness.

 In Webster's equipment as an orator we have first the splendid physical organization, which overwhelmed his auditory, and which we cannot well recall or reproduce. We have also to realize the intellectual qualities which we have already analyzed. In building his speeches Webster was always simple and straightforward. He instinctively sought the effective logical arrangement and seemed to develop his theme with the energy and directness of Nature herself. He had an astonishing gift for clarifying difficult problems and making them at any rate appear intelligible. His manner of statement was so impressive that it carried conviction, and surely no form of conviction is more enduring. It was often said that he stated the position of his opponents better than they could themselves, secure in his power later to rebut and overthrow it. His gift of narrative, of vividly portraying situations and characters, was admirable and unsurpassed.

But, when it comes to more purely literary quali-

16

ties, I feel some disappointment in reading Webster largely. He himself said at an early stage of his career: 'I resolved that, whatever else should be said of my style, from that time forth there should be no *emptiness* in it.' [8] The public speaker who could achieve this would go a long way. Webster's age was peculiarly the period of emptiness in American oratory, and to say that few are less chargeable with emptiness than he is saying a good deal. As regards style, he had color and amplitude. Yet it seems to me that the highest qualities of imagination, the qualities of Shakespeare and the great English poets and prose writers, are not very evident in him. Again, as to rhythm. Good critics maintain that the rhythm and swing of his sentences are superlative. I do not always find them so. Sometimes he gets a rhythm that sweeps you off your feet. More often I find in the words, as printed, an effort at harmony which is not quite successful, a rhythmic inadequacy, as compared with such masters as Milton and Landor.

All that shrewdness, quickness, aptness would do in speech, Webster always did. There was, of course, little room for humor in his published speeches; but when occasion called for it, he was ready and effective. His sarcasm is sometimes ponderous, but it is immensely powerful. Only, and it is to his credit, he rarely attacked individuals, and when he did, as with Ingersoll, in 1846, he kept it out of his printed works. Cicero's most splendid efforts are his bitter personal attacks on Catiline, Clodius, Verres, Antony. Webster had hardly occasion for such attacks, and in any case his spirit was too kindly.

Back of it all there remains this puzzling, inexplicable problem of the almost limitless power of spoken words, whether to afflict and bore, or to inspire and carry away. In this, as in other things, I find in Webster little tendency to analyze his own gift, either its sources, or its glory, or the infinite intoxication of exercising it. But I know no more vivid exhibition of what the power was than is contained in Hone's account of its display and effect on a very abnormal occasion: 'He rose at two o'clock in the morning, intending, in consequence of its being, as he said, *to-morrow*, to be very brief; but his auditors insisted upon his going on; they would not allow him to stop, and he, apparently "nothing loath," kept on in a strain of unwearied and unwearying eloquence until *four* o'clock. One hundred and fifty persons, most of them men of sober, steady habits, fathers of families, remained immovable in their seats, with no indications of fatigue or inattention, until he finished.' [9]

II

We can now watch the application of these elements of Webster's character in the chief points of his professional and political career. His technical activity as a lawyer is not always stressed as it might be; yet those who knew him well, like Choate, were of the opinion that his power nowhere appeared more impressively or effectively than in his arguments before a jury. Perhaps the most notable of his criminal cases were his prosecution of the murderers of Mr. White of Salem and the Goodridge case, in which with persistent energy and ingenuity he tracked down the man who had wounded himself and then endeavored to fix a charge of assault and robbery on others. In such cases as these he was especially noted for his power over witnesses, as is vividly suggested in Emerson's account of a particular instance: 'In Boston he looked a witness out of court — once, he set his great eyes on him, and searched him through and through; then, as the cause went on and this prisoner's perjury was not yet called for, he looked round on him to see if he was safe and ready for the inquisition he was preparing to inflict on him. The witness felt for his hat, and edged towards the door; a third time he looked on him, and the witness could sit no longer, but seized his opportunity, fled out of court, and could nowhere be found, such was the terror of those eyes.' [10] Also, he had a startling, bare intensity, in presenting the essentials of a dramatic situation, so that any jury would be impressed and convinced.

Even the arguments in civil cases, naturally less sensational in their quality, that in the Girard College case, with its religious implications, or such necessarily dryer treatments as the Providence Railroad versus the City of Boston, may be read to-day with instruction and sometimes with entertainment.

Webster's pleas before the Supreme Court in Washington, in broadly constitutional cases, have of course a more permanent significance than these more private issues. The first of importance was the Dartmouth College case, in 1818, in which Webster introduced his own personal feeling so intensely and effectively as to impart his emotion to the Court and to all the auditory: 'It is, as I have said, a small college, and yet there are those who love it.' The point in the case was to establish the

validity of the original college charter as inviolable
under the contract clause of the Constitution, and
the further bearing of this, as of so many of Webster's later arguments, was to broaden and solidify
the meaning, the significance, the national dignity
of the American Union. Sometimes Webster used
the firm, vigorous reasoning of John Marshall,
sometimes Marshall embodied Webster's views in
his own judicial opinions; but always they were
working toward the same end, to strengthen and
perpetuate the common interests and the common
power of a common country.

The same love of the Union and passionate desire
to maintain it appear in Webster's more general
speeches delivered on public historical occasions.
The most notable of these were the Plymouth
Speech, in 1820, the Eulogy of Jefferson and
Adams, in 1826, the Bunker Hill Speeches, in 1825
and 1843, and with these may be classed the speech
on Greek affairs, which, though delivered in Congress, was more generally historical in its nature.
Portions of these speeches are the best known
popularly of any of Webster's work. How overwhelming the effect of them was when delivered
may be appreciated from Ticknor's striking account
of his experience at Plymouth: 'I was never so

excited by public speaking before in my life. Three or four times I thought my temples would burst with the gush of blood. . . . When I came out, I was almost afraid to come near to him. It seemed to me as if he was like the mount that might not be touched and that burned with fire. I was beside myself and am so still.' [11]

When we come to consider Webster's political career, it is evident that he was not a largely, or elaborately, or persistently constructive statesman. His name is associated with very little in the way of definite development or modification of the American government. As a legislator, whether in the House or the Senate, his most valuable work was in connection with legal and judicial measures. As an administrator, during his Secretaryship of State under Tyler, he negotiated with Lord Ashburton the English treaty which settled the northern boundary, and to effect this he remained in the Cabinet after the resignation of his colleagues, bringing upon himself a good deal of undeserved odium by so doing. Professor Channing says that as the treaty was wholly pleasing to neither side, it may be assumed to represent a reasonable compromise. At any rate, it obviated war. Some of Webster's other official transactions were less

happy, though his later correspondence with Hülsemann was a vigorous and on the whole commend-
able assertion of national dignity. But if he is to be
regarded as one of the greatest builders and pre-
servers of the Union, perhaps other minor con-
struction should not be required of him.

As regards political measures and movements,
it may be urged that the circumstances of the times
and Webster's party and personal connections led
him to be often in opposition, and consequently
rather to criticize and thwart the activity of others
than to develop fruitful conceptions of his own. At
the same time, it must be recognized that very
often even his criticism was fruitful. His elucida-
tion of difficult topics and problems was so clear, so
intelligent, so masterly, that when he was opposing
he helped, and his exposition of all sorts of subjects
is permanently valuable for its lucid presentation
and suggestiveness.

This is especially true in regard to finance. He
himself said: 'The subject of currency, gentlemen,
has been the study of my life.' [12] Whether he was
discussing banks or bankruptcy, he had something
of Peel's or Gladstone's power of making complex
money questions interesting, and those who are
learned in such matters praise not only the wise

AS GOD MADE THEM

conservatism of his attitude, but his remarkable
gift of analyzing and synthesizing the most difficult
financial problems.

In the matter of the tariff his position is less
generally commended, and here we run across the
bugbear of consistency, so troublesome to most
statesmen who have long and active careers. In
early life Webster fought a high tariff, when the
South wanted it. Later, he shifted about, of course
with ingenious argument, and favored protection
for New England industries against the interests
of the South. The course was not only inconsistent,
in appearance at any rate, it was sectional, and
champions of the Southern cause argue energetically that Webster and his industrial New England
supporters really did more to split the Union than
the advocates of slavery. To most of us this appears exaggerated, and it cannot be questioned that
Webster, in intention at any rate, would have
swept all New England industry into the dustbin
rather than sacrifice the Union to maintain it. Or
he would have said that no industry and no prosperity anywhere were possible without the Union;
for more and more his passion for a united country
came to override his sectional interests and instincts of any kind whatever.

DANIEL WEBSTER

The first elaborate logical development of this love of the Union came in the speeches against Hayne, in 1830. This discussion originated when Foote of Connecticut introduced his Resolution in regard to Public Lands. Benton thereupon reproached New England with its selfish and encroaching industrialism, and Hayne supported these reproaches with ingenious reasoning for the constitutional right of secession. Hayne's arguments were able and forcible, as were those of his greater followers, Calhoun, Davis, and Stephens. Webster, in his earlier years, had sometimes appeared to take that side, and though not a member of the Hartford Convention, which carried New England protest almost to the point of revolt during the War of 1812, he was strongly opposed to the central administration at that time. After all, the Constitution was a compromise, cunningly framed to meet all sorts of prejudices, and it was possible to deduce very various conclusions from it. In the mere matter of logical metaphysics Webster did not always have the better of his opponents. What gave overwhelming power to his insistence upon the absolute necessity of a strong, dominating central government for the future and the welfare of America was the irresistible force of common-

25

sense that lay behind it, and common-sense always prevails over ingenious logic. Webster's position is effectively summed up in the sentences of General Lee, written shortly before he drew his sword in support of secession: 'Secession is nothing but revolution. . . . It is idle to talk of secession. Anarchy would have been established and not a government, by Washington, Hamilton, Jefferson, Madison, and the other patriots of the Revolution.' [13] The magnificent phrases of Webster did more than anything else to fix this truth in the heart of the North and West and in many Southern hearts also.

From 1830 on Webster's ardor for the Union was never shaken; but the situation grew more and more difficult, with the development of the Western country, the annexation of Texas, the Mexican War, and the violence of the Abolitionists arousing the energetic activity of the slave-holding South. Webster had always hated slavery and continued to hate it, but he believed that the natural movement of the modern world would destroy it in the end, and he held with Lincoln that the thing of paramount importance was to preserve the Union: sooner or later slavery must go anyway, but if the Union were once dissevered, the chances were that it would never be restored.

DANIEL WEBSTER

In 1850 the condition of things was critical. Henry Clay brought forward his elaborate Compromise measures, and after long deliberation Webster made his Seventh of March Speech in favor of them and did more than any one to insure their final passage. The Abolitionists called him traitor and renegade and did all they could to blacken his memory forever. This bitterness persists even in the 'Life' by Senator Lodge, written in 1883. But such investigations as those of Professor Foster, in *The American Historical Review*, prove conclusively how great the danger was, and how potent was Webster's influence in averting it. He may perhaps have shown some unnecessary irritation in his method of advocating the Fugitive Slave Law and in his comments on the Abolitionists, but his main activity was more than beneficent, it was vitally operative. From 1850 to 1860 the North far outstripped the South in growth, both as to numbers and as to wealth, and behind the North came in the growth and power of the West; yet even so, when the actual contest arrived, the North and West had all they could do to secure victory. It was owing to Clay, and most of all to Webster, that the Civil War was postponed for ten years, and therefore that we have one government of the United States of America, instead of two, or half a dozen, all tearing at each other, with the mutual jealousies, and the constant conflicts, and the ruinous standing armies that have always afflicted Europe.

III

When we turn to Webster's private and personal life, the complications were quite as subtle as in his public, and certainly quite as interesting. In his family he always had singular charm. His attachment to his father, and especially to his brother Ezekiel, is singularly winning, and Ezekiel's death was one of the severest blows that Daniel had to meet. His affection for his first wife, Grace, was also of a most tender and enduring quality. She seems, like the first Mrs. Woodrow Wilson, to have exercised a peculiarly favorable influence upon her husband's character and fortunes both, and some biographers have contrasted this influence with that of the second wife, Caroline LeRoy, who was much more a woman of the world, and of the world as Webster became more and more inclined to it. The deaths of four of his five children, all born of his first marriage, seemed to pile up affliction to a weight no worldly prosperity or success could counterpoise, and everything shows that Webster felt these losses poignantly. At the same time, if we may draw a delicate distinction, in all his emotions I should mark rather vivacity than intensity. His superficial sensitiveness was quick and acute, easily aroused and perhaps also easily dissipated. It does not appear that any emotional experience took a profoundly permanent hold upon him.

In the larger human relations he had the same charm and attractiveness as with his family. The lack of intense emotional experience indicated above perhaps prevented his having very intimate friendships, and as life went on, his human contacts were too widely distributed for such closer connection. He himself complains sadly: 'With a multitude of acquaintance, I have few friends.' [14] In general society he may have been a trifle too dignified for perfect ease. But with those who knew him well, he had extraordinary grace and power of sympathetic converse. Children turned to him, young people turned to him: he had in a high degree the valuable social gift of entering into others' lives.

All reporters tell us that Webster's talk was charming. He had his hours of depression and unresponsiveness. But when he liked his company, he could discourse with infinite profit and enter-

tainment on serious subjects and trivial alike. And
he let others talk and made them talk. Also, he had
a splendid supply of spirits and fun. Whether he
had the deeper humor of Lincoln or Lamb, the
humor which dissolves even one's self in insignificance, I greatly doubt: self was too big an object in
Webster's universe to be dissolved under any circumstances. But he had always an abundance of
the kindly jest and laughter, which can turn an
awkward circumstance into an amusing one and
can sometimes make even ugly things more toler-
able.

Webster's weaknesses have been largely amplified
by his enemies and somewhat painfully minimized
by his friends. One of the most marked and undeniable was personal finance. We have seen that
he boasted of his thorough knowledge of currency
in the abstract, but the current feature of money
was the one that chiefly affected his own pocket.
He looked more to glory and to public usefulness
than to profit, and he had not the gift some have of
making the two compatible. When he was quite
young, he refused a humble, fairly lucrative clerk-
ship, much against his father's wishes, because he
aimed at larger professional advancement. It was
said of him then that he did not know what money

was. Unfortunately he knew too much about the things that money buys, and had a keen appetite for most of them. He liked to spend, he liked to give, profusely, carelessly, and the money had to come from somewhere. His unpublished letters to his younger partner, Henry W. Kinsman, my grandfather, show constant money difficulties, as do his printed letters too frequently. His farms cost money, his entertaining cost money. As time went on, the difficulties and the indulgence increased. When he became important to his constituents, the wealthy manufacturers and merchants contributed to his support. This gave ground for all sorts of harmful charges. It is not for one moment to be supposed that Webster deliberately violated his political conscience; in private matters, as in the public affairs involved in Ingersoll's charges of corruption, the most that can be properly imputed is the confusion and disorder naturally incident to the finances of a man who 'never kept regular accounts or had them kept.' [15] But it is a profound remark of Webster himself that 'there are means of influence not generally esteemed positively corrupt, which are competent to produce great effects.' [16] And the chapter of personal finance is no more creditable to him than to some other public men of great influence and in the main high character. How some of his contemporaries felt about it is suggested in the bitter strictures contained in a private letter of Calhoun: 'Webster is regarded as the controlling spirit and he has become almost universally odious. There is no confidence in him. His integrity is questioned by almost all of any party.' [17]

Even better known than the money delinquencies are the charges against Webster's morals. He was constantly accused of intemperance. There is no doubt that he liked good living, and was a connoisseur in wines and food. When a strong man dies of cirrhosis of the liver, the suggestion of alcohol is apt to obtrude itself. It was a drinking age, and Webster can certainly claim no special abstemiousness. But the charges that he appeared in public and spoke when drunk have never been proved and are just the sort most readily circulated and most easily believed, as with Edwin Booth. To me Webster's love of the sunrise and habit of five o'clock in the morning work are quite inconsistent with serious dissipation.

Mr. Rhodes and many others have accused Webster of loose relations with women. More recent investigation of this subject seems to bring back the stories mainly to Abolitionist slander, at any rate fails to discover any definite evidence. That the somewhat Bohemian semi-bachelor life in Washington should have developed erratic tendencies in a man of Webster's temperament would neither astonish nor greatly distress one who was mainly interested in his public achievements.

I do not find anything in Webster's religion particularly discordant with his morals. He was a devout church member, frequently discoursed upon religious subjects, and always with gravity and infinite unction. I believe that he was perfectly sincere and that there was not a tinge of deliberate hypocrisy in all this. But I do not see the slightest evidence that religion ever took profound hold of him, either as a matter of agony or as a matter of rapture. I have an irresistible disposition to class his religion with his politics. God offered an excellent parallel to the Constitution, and the Bible took the place of the Supreme Court. The decrees of the one, when supported by the judicial rulings of the other, were to be accepted as final, beyond argument and above dispute. It was neither politic nor decorous to do anything else. The Christian universe, like the Union, must be maintained:

otherwise the consequences would be too horrible for contemplation.

One thing that helps out Webster from the moral point of view is the nature of his relaxations. He does not appear to have cared much for æsthetic interests. Music affected him little. He who spent money on many things did not spend much on pictures or ornaments. Even in literature his tastes were mainly rhetorical. He liked Shakespeare and Milton. He especially liked the eighteenth-century poets, in many respects he had an eighteenth-century mind. But the subtler poetry of his own day, Wordsworth, Shelley, Keats, did not attract his attention. He liked to speak orations and to read them, in various forms.

What he did above all enjoy and what from early manhood till past sixty kept him in splendid physical vigor, was the life out of doors. He did not indulge in romantic raptures about nature, or romantic melancholy. His much-praised descriptions of Niagara are external and rhetorical. He did not read Rousseau or Rousseau's followers. It does not appear that he did much scientific reading or thinking, though he liked to hold forth on such subjects. But he was an acute and careful observer by nature. He liked to wander all day with rod or gun, and

DANIEL WEBSTER

was a passionate sportsman. Yet he loved the birds
and animals for their life and vitality, as well as for
their deaths. He took the most intense interest in
the development of his great farms at Franklin and
at Marshfield, in his stock, in his crops, and his
letters to his farmers are among his most characteristic and attractive. These things ruined him finan-
cially, but they amused him. He liked all the large
aspects of the natural world, the sky, the sweep of
wide fields, above all, the sea. When he was worn
and torn with public and private anxiety and care,
he would wander alone along the beach at Marshfield, and it seemed to make him a new man. And
this does not sound to me like a debauchee or a
reprobate.

Yet, all through the farming and the shooting
and the fishing, as well as through the indolent,
tranquil social and domestic life, there was always
present or latent the passionate desire to do and be
something great in the world, and when Webster
went for a day's quiet trout fishing in the New
Hampshire brooks, the friend who was with him,
happening to look up, saw him strike an oratorical
attitude and murmur the beginning of his later address to the Veterans at Bunker Hill: 'Venerable
men.' It is amusing to see the effort of biographers

to minimize Webster's ambition. He sacrificed his personal welfare and inclinations, they say, for the benefit of his country and mankind. We get a far truer view in Plumer's evidently careful record of a conversation which took place of a moonlight night in the Capitol grounds, when Webster was forty years old: 'He broke out into the most passionate aspirations after glory. Without it life, he said, was not worth possessing. The petty struggles of the day were without interest to him, except as they might furnish the opportunity for doing or saying something which would be remembered in after time. . . . "I have done absolutely nothing. At thirty Alexander had conquered the world; and I am forty." Observing that I smiled at his enthusiasm, he smiled too; and said, "You laugh at me, Plumer! Your quiet way of looking at things may be the best, after all; but I have sometimes such glorious dreams! And sometimes, too, I half believe that they will one day wake into glorious realities."' [18]

The ambition of American statesmen usually bends toward the presidency, and there is no doubt that Webster's later years were filled with presidential aspirations. His Abolitionist enemies asserted that he threw away his past and his conscience to conciliate presidential support in the South by the Seventh of March Speech. This is absurd, and that speech is sufficiently justified by patriotic motives and patriotic results. But the hope of the presidency lingered to the very end, and Webster's disappointment at missing the Baltimore nomination in 1852 recalls the disappointment of Blaine forty years later.

As the red thread of ambition runs through all the tissue of Webster's character, so I think we may discern also, more and more in later years, the tinge of the orator, the suggestion of pose, and a certain artificial dignity, which had to be preserved always. The oratorical attitude, with the hand thrust into the breast of the frock coat, which afflicted stump speakers for a generation, seems to be the natural guise in which to think of Webster, and it belonged to his soul as well as to his outer man

Little touches significant of this could be gathered everywhere from Webster's own words and those of his biographers, but the most admirable illustration of it is the death scene, so faithfully recorded by Curtis, but strangely neglected by biographers since. Everybody knows the very last words, 'I still live,' striking words certainly, and significant of an intense vitality struggling with the gathering shadows of oblivion. But to me there is far more depth of humanity, in fact a concise epitome of the man, in the speech uttered a few hours earlier. When death seemed imminent, Webster made sure that all his household were assembled, and Curtis, seeing that something impressive was coming, settled himself with ink and paper, so that not a word might be lost or inexact. The dying orator then delivered a senatorial address on general religious topics, of the rather futile and rhetorical order usual in his remarks on such subjects, though there is one superb touch, when he declares that the ancients had 'crepuscular — twilight' intimations of immortality. How the dying nerves must have throbbed and thrilled at the felicitous hit of 'crepuscular'! The effort of this speech was too much for him, and his eyes closed. When he came to himself again, he looked about eagerly, and exclaimed: 'Have I — wife, son, doctor, friends, are you all here? — have I, on this occasion, said anything unworthy of Daniel Webster?' [19] I do not know many things in history that will beat that for concentrated human truth. Try to apply that speech to other notable men. Chatham might have been capable of it. Napoleon, just possibly, though with his tongue in his cheek. But who can imagine Lincoln staging such a performance, who can imagine Shakespeare? Shakespeare would have smiled and said, 'nothing human can be unworthy of Shakespeare.' In all the crepuscular utterances of mortality I know of none more magnificent: 'Have I — wife, son, doctor, friends, are you all here? — have I, on this occasion, said anything unworthy of Daniel Webster?' And then there comes the due wail of Greek choral response: 'No, no, dear sir.' 'No, no, dear sir.' And the drama is complete.

IV

As a whole, I think we may sum up Webster most effectively by emphasizing the Anglo-Saxon, or the plain Englishman, in him. In many American types, even those directly derived from English stock, there seems to be marked variation, partly owing to a selected strain in the original immigrant, partly to climate, partly to surrounding conditions and circumstances. Take Franklin, take Jefferson, take Emerson, take Mark Twain, take Lincoln preëminently, they all seem to have something in them which we call American as distinguished from the pure English. In Webster we do not note this: he was Anglo-Saxon all over, which may account in part for the comparative indifference to him in recent years.

Consider the various manifestations of the impress of the Anglo-Saxon in him. Take physique. Emerson, Mark Twain, Lincoln, were distinctly American types. Webster's burly, sturdy, massive chest and shoulders seem thoroughly English. Take his out-of-door life. He meant to be democratic, and thought he was. He early and largely employed the cant about labor which has brought success to so many American politicians. But his farmers called him 'Squire,' and evidently he liked it. His instinctive ideal was the English country gentleman, surrounded and looked up to by his tenants and dependents, not the simple American man among his fellows. It is the same with morals: respectability, decorum, propriety must be preserved, no matter what went on underneath. It was not deliberate hypocrisy, it was just wholesome convention. And the religion was convention in the same way: a conventional creed, a conventional church, a conventional God, as far removed from profound thinking on the one hand as from mystical rapture on the other. Above all, Webster was Anglo-Saxon in politics, wisely, largely, intelligently, practically conservative. Things as they were were not so bad, and they should be kept as they were, or changed and modified only with extreme care and patient adjustment. Especially English is the insistence upon property. Property is prudence, character, respectability, it might almost be said that property is virtue. 'It would seem, then, to be the part of political wisdom to found government on property.' [20] And in taking part in the remodeling of the Massachusetts Constitution, Webster energetically urged a property franchise as indispensable.

So, in his rapturous visions of the future and the expansion and the power and the greatness of America, it was always an English America that he foresaw: 'Now, Gentlemen, I do not know what practical views or what practical results may take place from this great expansion of the power of the two branches of Old England. It is not for me to say. I only can see, that on this continent *all* is to be *Anglo-American*, from Plymouth Rock to the Pacific seas, from the North Pole to California.' [21] Liberty, prosperity, and futurity were bound up with English descent: 'Human liberty may yet, perhaps, be obliged to repose its principal hopes on the intelligence and vigor of the Saxon race.' [22]

At the same time, it must not be for a moment supposed that Webster indulged in any cheap form of Anglomania, cultivated English speech, or dress, or manners, with any of the affectation that appears in even such genuine Americans as Sumner and Lowell. He was too big for that. He was born an American, he lived and died an American, and nothing else. It was simply that his America was wholly an English America, and in his wide imagination he saw its future as that of a magnified and glorified England. The vast complexity of stocks and ideals which has developed since his day, and which knows little of an English inheritance and inclines to hold that little in contempt, was out of his vision altogether. Yet, for all that, he was American through and through, and would have been so under all circumstances and changing conditions. He kept the Stars and Stripes flying day and night at the masthead of his little yacht; while life was in his body, he kept them flying in his heart. And so long as these States hold together in a unified government, so long as the Stars and Stripes float over a great American Republic, so long should the citizens of that Republic, of whatsoever origin or creed, remember that few men did more to establish or maintain their country than Daniel Webster.

II
HENRY CLAY

CHRONOLOGY

HENRY CLAY

Born, Hanover County, Virginia, April 12, 1777.

1792–1797, legal work and preparation in Richmond.

Removed to Kentucky, 1797.

Married Lavinia Hart, 1799.

First appearance in United States Senate, 1806.

Speaker of House of Representatives, 1811.

Commissioner to Ghent, 1814.

Advocated Missouri Compromise, 1820.

Supported John Quincy Adams for President, 1825.

Secretary of State, 1825–1829.

Arranged tariff compromise, 1833.

Active in Bank struggle, 1833–1834.

Retired from Congress, 1842.

Candidate for President, 1844.

Arranged Compromise in Senate, 1850.

Died, Washington, June 29, 1852.

HENRY CLAY

HENRY CLAY

I

OF the three great American political figures of the second quarter of the nineteenth century who are commonly grouped together, Henry Clay seems to be the most distinctly and warmly human. Calhoun grew to be more and more a creature of logic. His intellect crushed his passions, though in such cases the passions have queer ways of revenging themselves. Webster was human enough in his own nature; but the rest of mankind never seemed quite to touch him. He understood them, you may say he loved them, but he went his lofty, indifferent way, without too much regard to them, and they paid him back in kind. Clay was human all through, lived, throbbed, thrilled in the contact of humanity. Many men loved him. Some men hated him. All felt that he was a man like themselves. He felt it also, liked to feel it, and strove and aspired to make a mighty, vital nation out of common human passions and struggles and hopes.

Henry Clay was born April 12, 1777, in the 'Slashes,' Hanover County, Virginia. His father died when the boy was small, and his mother married again. Henry knocked about Richmond in his youth, and finally, through the most helpful protection of Chancellor Wythe, made his way to a legal education. He then followed his mother to Kentucky, in 1797, and began practice there. He was soon and decidedly successful, not only in law, but in politics. He was sent to the United States Senate in 1806, when slightly under the legal age. He afterwards entered the House and immediately became Speaker. He was one of the most active promoters of the War of 1812. With Adams, Gallatin, and others, he negotiated the peace at Ghent. Returning to Congress, he took a prominent part in the Missouri Compromise of 1820. As Speaker, in 1825, he was the chief influence in giving the disputed presid tial election to John Quincy Adams, and afterwards became Secretary of State, thus affording his enemies a disastrous chance to accuse him of corrupt bargaining. He was a candidate for presidential nomination or election in nearly every campaign for twenty-five years, but failed to get the prize, in spite of his immense personal popularity. In 1833, after having for years advocated a high tariff, he effected a moderate compromise in this regard, and so averted the Nullification crisis. He fought Jackson as to the Bank and in other ways, and was beaten. He was defeated by Harrison for the presidency in 1840, by Polk in 1844, by Taylor in 1848. In 1850 he closed his career with the great achievement of the slavery compromise, and he died June 29, 1852.

We shall best get at Clay and the significance of his large humanity by taking him from within outward and beginning with him in his home. His inner personal life seems to have been unimportant, at least so far as any of the extensive records show. He had the very elementary education of a common school in Virginia in that day, and added little to it later, except by his own facility and shrewdness of apprehension. Even his law he picked off the bushes, as it were. It was a thing of shreds and tatters, woven together by the astonishing aptitude of an eager and ambitious spirit, but never remarkable for profundity or substance. He read fairly widely, though in the main history and politics, with a little poetry, and he retained a good deal of what might be useful to him, but nothing in his life or writing shows much thought given to general questions, not even legal, not even political. One who knew him well says, 'He had no knowledge of the metaphysics or rhetoric or logic of the schools, and in fact had a hearty contempt for all three of them.' [1] Perhaps it would have been better if the contempt had been a little less hearty.

Of the influence of æsthetic emotion there is no sign whatever in Clay. If music or painting meant anything to him, we are not told of it: he makes not the remotest allusion to such matters in his extensive private correspondence. Nor does natural beauty appear to have had any such hold on him as it had on Webster. Clay loved his great Kentucky estate at Ashland, and felt the charm of its fine old trees and rolling meadows. But his interest in it was mainly agricultural, after all. And of analysis of his own inner experience in these concerns there is very little trace. Clay's letters are more barren in this regard than even Webster's, and this is saying a good deal. These men were so immensely preoccupied with what went on in the world about them that they had little attention for what went on within. Perhaps they were happier and more useful for this very reason, but the neglect sometimes led to curious results.

As to Clay's immediate personal relations, nothing is told us of any early love affairs or of more intimate relations with women. Women always liked and admired him at all periods of his life, and he liked them. If they had been voting in his day, he would have been President without a question. He was a favorite on social occasions, and would seem likely to have had amorous entanglements. Political scandal flaunted various anecdotes of sexual irregularity; but the faithful Kentucky biographer tells us that he has investigated these and found no basis for them, and we must accept his statement, since we cannot do better, or worse.[2]

In any case, Clay married young, a cousin of Senator Benton, Lavinia Hart, who had social standing and some means, and the marriage was a happy one. Mrs. Clay had numerous children and watched over her husband's establishment with devoted care. I do not find that she was much help to him politically: she seems to have had neither political ambition nor remarkable social graces. The only trace of her interest in public matters is that, after the defeat in 1844, 'Mrs. Clay took him in her arms, and said, as they wept together: "My husband, this ungrateful people can never truly appreciate you while living."' [3] But she was an excellent housekeeper, and more than that, a faithful, sympathetic, responsive wife and mother. Clay's few letters to her that have been preserved are as conventional as Webster's in the same connection, but I find one little touch in them that has a depth of human significance. He is expressing a due sorrow for her absence and her loneliness, and he adds (italics mine): 'I regret it extremely, and, *whatever you may think to the contrary*, I should have preferred greatly your accompanying me.'[4] The absences were frequent, however, and indeed the husband finally died in Washington, when his wife was far away.

Mr. and Mrs. Clay had a patriarchal family, five sons and six daughters. Clay was singularly fond of children; not only loved them but understood them, and they loved him. Charming stories are told of his devotion to his little granddaughters, and Mrs. Smith's account of his grief over the loss of an infant is pathetic.[5] But, like Webster, he was tragically unsuccessful in bringing up his family. One of the sons became insane from an accident and was a constant sorrow. Another was killed in the Mexican War. And every one of the six daughters died before her father. Ann, Mrs. Erwin, was an especial favorite and the account of Clay's distress at hearing of her death is characteristic of his intensely sensitive and nervous temperament. 'Poor Mr. Clay,' says Mrs. Smith, 'was laughing and talking and joking with some friends when his papers and letters were brought to him; he naturally first

opened the letter from home. A friend who was
with him says he started up and then fell as if shot
and his first words were, "Every tie to life is
broken." . . . Ann was his pride as well as his joy
and of all his children his greatest comfort.' [6]

Yet it is curious to note how the habit of the
rhetorician and the instinct of publicity prevail and
intertwine themselves with even the most intimate
personal emotions. Goethe said that whenever he
had a sorrow he made a poem. When Clay had a
sorrow he made a speech. After one of his domestic
misfortunes, he went North to seek distraction, and
when a receiving committee of entire strangers
visited him, this is the extraordinary way in which
he expressed himself: 'I could not look upon the
partner of my sorrows without feeling deeper
anguish. [The speaker was here overcome by his
feelings, and paused some minutes, covering his
face with his hands.] . . . Of eleven children four
only now remain [great emotion]. Of six lovely
daughters not one is left. Finding myself in the
theater of sadness, I thought I would fly to the
mountain's top and descend to the ocean's wave,
and by meeting with the sympathy of friends obtain some relief for the sadness which surrounds
me.' [7]

Clay's humanity appears in his relation with his slaves as in other things. He suffered from the same conflict of feelings that affected so many of the earlier slaveholders until Calhoun and his followers argued themselves free from it. Clay always regarded slavery as an evil and a curse for every one and he was an ardent advocate of getting rid of it by colonization; yet habit enabled him to live with it comfortably and profit by it. When the Quaker Mendenhall visited him and begged him to free his slaves, he pointed out the numerous difficulties and incidentally asked whether the Quaker's supporters were prepared to pay the fifteen thousand dollars that such a sacrifice would cost. But if we may trust his own evidence and that of others, he always treated his slaves with gentleness and consideration and was beloved by them in return. His body-servant Charles was more a friend than a slave, and when they traveled together in the Northern States and efforts were made to get Charles to leave his master, Clay laughed and said: 'You may have him, if you can get him.' [8]

In the management of his domestic finances, Clay was prudent and careful, had none of Webster's happy-go-lucky indifference, and was consequently never for a moment liable to the charges that were brought against Webster. Clay had to struggle with poverty in his youth and was proud of it. He made a fortune by his own efforts and might have made much more if politics had not engrossed him. He was most exact and systematic in accounts and in discharging all obligations, though his large estate, his profuse hospitality, and especially his readiness to help others and his easiness in undertaking their obligations did at one time involve him in serious difficulties, from which he was extricated by the generosity of quite unknown friends.

He was a practical farmer, took a great and constant interest in the development of his estate at Ashland, and especially devoted himself to animals, above all to the breeding of the beautiful Kentucky horses. When he was in Washington, he sighed for Ashland, though it is no doubt true that, with the charming inconsistency of human nature, when he was at Ashland, he sighed for Washington. The farm would have been much more costly and less successful than it was, if it had not been for the watchful assistance of Mrs. Clay, who, with eleven children on her hands, looked after every detail of the outdoor management and saved her husband trouble and money. As one relative says: 'It is related of Mrs. Clay that preparatory to her husband's departure from home, she invariably received from him a handsome check, which she as regularly restored to him upon his return, with the laconic remark that she had found no use for it.'[9] No doubt some American wives are like this, but others are not.

Clay's money was, of course, made in his profession of law and in this profession he was immensely successful. He himself says of the law: 'Two words will make any man of sound intellect a lawyer, industry and application, and the same words with a third, economy, will enable him to make a fortune.'[10] But I am inclined to think that two other elements entered more largely still into Clay's own success. The first was his vast knowledge of human nature and instinctive sympathy. Criminals, judges, juries, witnesses, and spectators, all came within his careful ken, and he adapted himself to them all with understanding and profit. And then he had his gift of speech. What that was we can only conjecture now from the stammering report of others; but evidently it was very remarkable and of the utmost value. He had no such oratorical physique as Webster. He was plain in feature, with a huge mouth, so large that, as he himself complained, he could never learn to spit, long and lanky in figure, with just a suggestion of the grotesqueness of Lincoln. But enthusiastic auditors mainly agree that when he spoke, he was all on fire and carried every one who heard away with him. A theme that touched his heart flashed and sparkled from his eyes, his 'catamount eyes,' [11] piped, or rolled, or thundered from his tongue, till the hearers utterly forgot themselves in sympathetic ardor. What they carried away permanently may not always have been very great, but for the time he swayed them at his will with overcoming emotion.

Perhaps the eloquence and the success were more marked in the romantic atmosphere of Kentucky than before the Supreme Court at Washington. Clay's pleadings before the latter tribunal are not preserved for us with the care that has been accorded to Webster's and they probably did not deserve it. In Kentucky he was especially fortunate in defending criminals, though he undertook no cause in which he did not see if not innocence, at least extenuation. It is said that no criminal defended by him ever suffered the extreme penalty of the law. When it came to Washington, on the other hand, we have the comment of Webster: 'The fact is, he was no lawyer. He was a statesman, a politician, an orator, but no reasoner.' [12] Yet Judge Story, surely an excellent authority, wrote: 'Your friend Clay has argued before us with a good deal of ability; and if he were not a candidate for higher offices, I should think he might attain great eminence at this Bar. But he prefers the fame of popular talents to the steady fame of the Bar.' [13]

We may complete the study of Clay's more personal life by a reference to his relations with God. Through most of his career these relations may be said to have been cordial but not intimate. One of his biographers points out that in those days the ideal of the religious life was so high that many men preferred to give their active years to this world and to save religion for the period of decline, or, as another charmingly puts it in regard to Clay: 'His life having been devoted so intensely to the good of others as scarcely, until this period of retirement, to leave him an opportunity to think of himself.' [14] Clay at all times referred to religious matters with the utmost decorum, and though his speech was sometimes addicted to profanity, his spirit was not. But as the grave came nearer, it seemed wise to take things a little more seriously, and at seventy, after much reverent discussion and inquiry, he became a member of the Episcopal Church. It appeared that he had never been baptized, and this point was, of course, attended to before confirmation. The ceremony was performed in the family parlor with the aid of a huge cut-glass vessel, which had been presented to the statesman some years before. No biographer hints at such a thing, but it seems to me highly probable that the vessel was a punch-bowl. It could hardly have been meant to hold flowers, and it certainly was not intended for a baptismal font. Baptized at seventy in a punch-bowl! Could there be a more delightful epitome of Kentucky life a century ago? Another attractive touch is that Clay is said to have murmured, 'Now I lay me down to sleep,' the night before he died, and to have repeated the same prayer every night of his life.[15] This accords exactly with the childlike candor and simplicity of so many of these great men of affairs and active interests. I cannot imagine Goethe or Sainte-Beuve or Darwin going to bed with 'Now I lay me'; yet perhaps they did.

II

Clay's humanness appears even more in his larger relations with humanity. He was a social being, and liked all sorts of people in all sorts of places. Webster, who was himself not averse to society, criticized Clay in this regard: 'He has been too fond of excitement — he has lived upon it; he has been too fond of company, not enough alone; and has had few resources within himself.' [16] It was said that Clay was dominant in any company. It was said that he liked to be, and some complained that his dominance was trying. It is certain that he had no shyness, never felt awkward or ill at ease, and by no means suffered from any inferiority complex. At the same time, he had so much cordial grace of manner and such quick, sympathetic response, that his self-assertion did not interfere with his extraordinary popularity.

He was always hospitable, and both at Ashland and in Washington liked to have numbers at his table and under his roof. Ticknor tells us in regard to that period: 'The truth is, that at Washington society is the business of life.' [17] This was an atmosphere that suited Clay exactly and he never failed to profit by it, both for ambition and for pleasure. He was an admirable and fluent talker, and the skill and control and adaptability that he had been able to attain are well indicated in Miss Martineau's account of him: 'Mr. Clay, sitting

upright on the sofa, with his snuff-box ever in his
hand, would discourse for many an hour, in his
even, soft, deliberate tone, on any one of the great
subjects of American policy which we might happen to start, always amazing us with the moderation of estimate and speech which so impetuous a nature has been able to attain.' [18] But it is positively
stated that Clay did not always do all the talking,
but that he was most skillful at questioning, drawing out others, and making them feel that they were
of importance. There is the narrative of the young
journalist, who spent a delightful hour with him in
a hotel at Saratoga, while Clay was dressing. Clay
quietly and deftly turned the boy's soul inside out
and left him fascinated. When he told Thurlow
Weed about it afterward, the old man laughed, and
said: 'Yes, that was like Henry: he always sent
everybody from him charmed, because he made
them think he was charmed with them.' [19] Surely
there is no better road to popularity than this.

One of Clay's attractions is his humor. As with
Webster, this humor has certainly not the depth or
penetration of Lincoln's. The older statesman was
too self-engrossed and not sufficiently analytical
for that. But, like Webster, he had a play of genial
fun which was useful for dispelling acrimony and

for somehow making tense situations lose their tension. He had also a remarkably apt quickness of tongue, which hit on just the poignant, pungent word at the right time. A much smaller man had taken his hat by mistake and had been forced to wear it down Pennsylvania Avenue. 'It looked like an extinguisher on me,' complained the man. 'You mean a distinguisher?' [20] said Clay. And undeniably the tongue was too often tempted to sting and would leave scars which reminded the victim of a hostility that might otherwise have been forgotten. Captain Marryat was a guest at Clay's table and they had a dispute about some minor matter. Clay, to smooth it over, invited his guest to drink with him. 'No,' answered Marryat roughly, 'I have had enough.' Clay turned to a younger man and diverted the invitation to him, adding, 'I see you have not had too much.' [21] And Marryat was not likely to forget it. Similar incidents in the Senate were long remembered.

I do not find much sign of Clay's taking part in out-of-door sports or social amusements. No doubt he shot and fished, but he can hardly have done it with the passion of Webster. He is said to have been a good swimmer and to have enjoyed it.[22] He could not have been a Kentuckian without be-

ing an excellent rider, and his love for race-horses
must have meant a love for racing and all the excitement it brings with it.

But indoor social diversions were his delight and
his temptation all his life. He liked the minor in-
cidental features of them. He liked a good dinner,
and especially the good drink that went with it. It
is not to be supposed that dissipation ever seriously
interfered with his capacity for work. When he had
had a late night of riotous entertainment, a friend
said to him, 'How can you, under the circumstances, preside over the House to-day?' 'Come
and see,' said Clay. The friend went and saw and
was satisfied.²³ Still, these things were distracting.
When you drink and smoke and take snuff cordially
with everybody, your inner life is apt to be somewhat neglected.

Above all, Clay relished the social stimulus of
cards. In his youth he was an eager and enthusiastic gambler. He liked to play brag, the earlier
equivalent of poker. The precise John Quincy
Adams, who never knew how to amuse himself, records with disgust that during the conferences of
the Commissioners at Ghent, who were settling the
affairs of the world, the card players could be heard
leaving Mr. Clay's room in the early hours of the

morning.[24] It is said that Clay once lost eight thousand dollars at a sitting and then kept on till he had won it all back except a hundred. In later years he gave up the more extreme forms of play, though he always delighted in whist. At one time he made a public avowal of regret for his dissipations. And his biographer tells us that a card was never seen at Ashland.[25] But what pleases me most in this connection is the story of Mrs. Clay and the lady from New England, because it so clearly marks the difference of climates and manners. This demure, Puritanic individual said to Mrs. Clay, 'Isn't it a pity your husband gambles so much?' And Mrs. Clay quietly replied: 'Oh, I don't know. He usually wins.' [26]

Probably few men meet and know so many people of all sorts as Clay did. It might almost be said that he lived in the life of others, or, perhaps more properly, that he drew the lives of all others into his own. Among this vast multitude he had many devoted friends, who gave him a warm and tender affection and received as much in return. He had, even more than Webster, the extraordinary memory for names and faces which is so apt to accompany great political success, and he remembered not only men's faces, but their affairs, inquired about their little concerns and could refer to them afterwards. This is well indicated in Dyer's account of Clay's way of receiving strangers: 'Clay would at once begin to talk with Jorkins about affairs in Jorkinsville. He would remember everybody he had ever met from Jorkinsville; or he might have passed through that region years before, and in that case he would have a vivid recollection of the country and its inhabitants. And he would send messages by Jorkins to all his old friends in Jorkinsville, and of course when Jorkins got home, he lost no time in delivering the messages in order to let his neighbors know that he had been with Henry Clay in Washington.' [27] Similar methods made a large element later in the popularity of Blaine, and the man who employs them is almost sure to be loved. And Clay not only talked cordially, he acted so. He was ready and thoughtful in doing kindnesses. Until harsh experience taught him the folly of it, he was always willing to indorse a friend's note, and surely greater love hath no man than this: laying down one's life is nothing in comparison.

It is especially interesting to observe how Clay's personal attraction entered into his relations with even those whose temperament was different, or who were actually hostile. It was easy to quarrel with that quick and bitter tongue; it was not easy to keep up the enmity. The case of Benton is significant. He was a cousin of Mrs. Clay's, and was often at the house. At times he and Clay acted cordially together. But their politics pulled them apart, and in the Senate they abused each other with a whole-heartedness that seemed to threaten bloodshed. Yet Benton continued to speak of his foe with consideration and esteem, and sometimes with tenderness. Even more interesting is the relation with Adams. No two men could be more different. In the Ghent negotiations they were often at odds, and Adams, in his diary and letters, speaks of Clay with the sharpest criticism. Yet when they worked together for four years, as President and Secretary of State, the record seems to be all harmony and mutual respect, and I know no finer testimony anywhere to Clay's personal qualities than this. Again, there were the two great rivals, Webster and Calhoun. Their political action was often in the most acute divergence from Clay's, and they were always contestants for the greatest office of all. Both Webster and Calhoun could depreciate their competitor at need; yet it is clear that they loved him, even while they hated him.

HENRY CLAY

Of course Clay had his enemies, many and bitter ones, whom no good-nature could conciliate, and no concessions or compromises could appease. Foremost among these was Andrew Jackson. There were certain resemblances between the two, which did not diminish the hostility. Both represented the people, though in very different aspects. Both represented the West, and were eager to represent it. Both were arbitrary, autocratic, anxious to rule. At an early stage it looked as if the country had not room for both of them. They came into conflict after conflict, and it must be confessed that on the whole Jackson came out ahead.

The natural hostility blazed up when Clay, in 1825, gave his vote and his influence to make Adams President instead of Jackson. Jackson's fierce prejudice seized upon the idea that here was a corrupt bargain, and Clay's appointment as Secretary of State seemed damning evidence of the fact. Clay honestly preferred Adams and his action was legitimate, but it was probably not wise, and it certainly haunted him like a ghost of defeat and disaster forever after. Jackson had the ear of the people and their hearts, and that cry of the corrupt bargain thwarted Clay's ambition for the rest of his life.

Furthermore, it was taken up, with his usual grotesqueness, by John Randolph, who was perhaps a greater enemy of Clay than of any one except of himself. Randolph's reported bitter taunt about the corrupt combination of Puritan and blackleg, of Blifil and Black George, plagued Clay beyond endurance and finally forced him to the last resort of a duel.

Duels were a weak point with Clay, as with so many Southerners. He could not defend them in principle, deplored them and believed that they would disappear 'when all shall unite, as all ought to unite, in their proscription.' [28] Meantime, he fought them when necessary. He had one with Marshall, in Kentucky, moderately bloodless. The one with Randolph was as picturesque as was everything concerning that erratic personage. He came on the ground in a white wrapper worn under his cloak. He discharged his pistol too soon through nervousness. He told Benton beforehand that he would not fire at Clay, then took one shot at him, then fired a second in the air. After it was over, he exchanged cordial greetings with him. Benton, who describes the whole performance with infinite serious relish, closes his narrative with this admirable comment: 'About the last high-toned duel that

HENRY CLAY

I have witnessed and among the highest-toned that I have ever witnessed.' [29]

Yet even Randolph, through it all, kept admiration, if not affection, for Clay: one of the Virginian's last public utterances was an expression of belief in the Kentucky statesman's ability to 'save the Union.' [30] And if even his enemies praised him, what shall be said of the immense popularity that he developed and retained among the masses of people? It is true that the popularity did not always work to practical ends, and one of Clay's supporters bitterly complained that he 'could get more men to run after him to hear him speak, and fewer to vote for him than any man in America.' [31] There were various and complicated reasons for this. But the popularity remains simple and unquestionable. It shows, as it showed with Blaine, in the familiar nicknames that passed from mouth to mouth, 'Harry of the West,' 'The Mill-Boy of the Slashes.' It shows in the immense enthusiasm which met him everywhere when he traveled over the country; and the enthusiasm warmed his heart and thrilled his sensitive nerves again and again to renewed ambition and hope. Others might be praised and listened to and followed and elected; this man was loved. And when you study his career,

you cannot but feel the force of the words of so
sober a critic as Rhodes: 'No man has been loved as
the people of the United States loved Henry Clay.' [32]

III

The foundation of Clay's political activity and
success, as in other things, was again the humanness. He had an intensely sensitive, nervous, high-
strung temperament. Mrs. Smith, who knew him
well, says, 'Excitement is as necessary to his moral
as stimulus is to his physical nature.' [33] Another
intimate friend emphasizes the same characteristic:
'His chief physical peculiarity, however, was in
the structure of his nervous system: it was so deli-
cately strung, that a word, a touch, a memory,
would set it in motion.' [34] And this sensibility was
always bent to enter into the lives and hearts of
others, to understand them, to work with them, to
benefit them, and naturally to benefit by them. He
was a creature of hopes and fears, of enthusiasms
and discouragements. At one moment a fiery ardor
swept him away and others along with him. Then
failure would bring depression and disgust. And
rest and fresh stimulus and new points of view
would set the wheels going again with more energy
than ever.

HENRY CLAY

The great instrument of political success was, of course, the oratory, the extraordinary power of speech. The reading of dead political speeches is tedious work, and I have been pretty well surfeited with them. Yet I have found Clay's better than I expected. I looked for rhetoric, for a rather sophomoric effusiveness. Clay has not perhaps the solid substance of Webster. But his speeches are not cheap rhetoric by any means. They are often terse, business-like, and to the point. His enthusiasm and lack of really solid study often led him to make wild statements, inaccurate estimates, prophecies that have ludicrously failed of realization. But he is generally simple and always sincere. Lincoln was an admirer and follower of Clay, and in Lincoln's eulogy of him there is one sentence, notable for its estimate of the subject and still more as being characteristic of the eulogist: 'He never spoke merely to be heard. He never delivered a Fourth-of-July oration, or a eulogy on an occasion like this.' [35] The praise is somewhat exaggerated, but it is in the main just. And whenever Clay does indulge in rhetoric, there is a certain warm-heartedness, a buoyant, boyish genuineness about it that makes the artificiality comparatively harmless.

But it is evident that the power and the effect of

the oratory did not lie wholly or largely in the words as we now read them in cold print. Men were swayed, carried away, swept right out of themselves by the magic of that infectious personality, the ardor, the magnetism, the fury of the gestures, above all by the subtle, penetrating music of the voice. To be sure memory may to some extent have exaggerated these things. I find in the manuscript letters of a kinsman of mine, written from Mississippi, in 1820, when Clay should have been at the height of his power, this description, which is hardly as enthusiastic as some others: 'His manner is rude, entirely without polish, and the man himself dresses and looks like a ploughman, but his eloquence is rapid, unstudied, without affectation, vehement, strong and logical, his voice is good, his undertones remarkably smooth and pleasant. Yet I was somewhat disappointed, probably because my expectations were so great.' The general testimony as to the effect of Clay's speaking, however, is too strong to be resisted or overlooked. For the time he made his audiences think as he did, even if the impression did not last. There is the story of the Jacksonian Democrat who did not care to occupy his seat in the House: 'Gentlemen,' he said, 'I was sent here to support Jackson and fight Clay. I have been instructed by the Legislature and warned from the White House. I am willing to do my duty when I can, but I'm d——d if I can listen to Henry Clay speak and believe he is wrong.' [36] And there is Lincoln's account of the effect of one speech, now, perhaps fortunately, lost: 'During its delivery the reporters forgot their vocation, dropped their pens, and sat enchanted from near the beginning to quite the close. The speech now lives only in the memory of a few old men, and the enthusiasm with which they cherish their recollection of it is absolutely astonishing.' [37] The memory of the old men does not so much impress me, but to enchant a reporter is indeed an achievement.

It must not be supposed, however, that Clay was all words. He could work when he chose, and work hard. His lack of early education and his imaginative ardor made him appear somewhat unreliable. But when he had a special case to get up, either legal or political, he could devote himself to it with a great amount of forgetfulness and industry.[38] As a member of Congress, he was rather notable for constructive work and for the quantity of statutory legislation which he fathered.[39] He himself declared that he had 'an unaffected repugnance to any executive employment'; [40] yet, when he was Secretary of

State, he got through a great deal of irksome detail, and it is said, with what truth I know not, that the number of treaties he concluded 'is greater than all which had ever been previously concluded from the first adoption of the Constitution.' [41] Especially notable in the matter of practical management is his Speakership. In the first place there is the extraordinary fact that he was elected Speaker on the very day of his appearance in the House, it was said because he was the only man who could bridle John Randolph. Also, in his long occupancy of the office he was triumphantly successful. He was just, reasonable, quick, energetically decided, and thoroughly expeditious in transacting business. He was probably the first to establish the great, if not wholly beneficial power of the Speaker, and he was the worthy predecessor of such able and highly esteemed autocrats as Blaine and Reed.

But it was as the leader of the Whig Party for many years that Clay was most conspicuous and will be most remembered. He was a born manager of men, had in the highest degree the gift of influencing them, persuading them, making them see things as he did, and this was accomplished not by trickiness or by sleight of hand, but by ardor and sincerity. No doubt he had the defects of such a temperament. He was too dominant, arbitrary, dictatorial, and this grew upon him, as of all defects it is most inclined to do. His enemies complained of his insolence and arrogance, and while his friends did not complain, they sometimes found these things irksome. Yet even when they groaned and doubted, they followed: his power was overwhelming and irresistible.

It is touching and pathetic to see the childlike innocence with which Clay disclaims the unwillingness to accept the leadership of others: 'Of all men upon earth am I the least attached to the productions of my own mind. No man upon earth is more ready than I am to surrender anything which I have proposed and to accept in lieu of it anything which is better.' [42] The world at large did not agree with him. Yet one should always remember his elaborate achievements in the way of compromise and also those four years of complete harmony and subordination with John Quincy Adams, who was not an easy man to follow. Clay got on with Adams, and admired him, and held Adams's affection to the end. To me it is the most remarkable fact in his career.

It is the more remarkable because of the evident ardor of his personal ambition, although even here it might be urged that in temporary adherence to Adams ambition saw its clearest road to success. With Clay, as with Webster, and with most, if not all other great statesmen, it is curious to observe the endless play of self-deceived ambition, as it alternately denies and reasserts itself. Clay proclaims over and over again that he is not ambitious. He is only seeking the good of his country. If his country requires his services, no matter how distinguished the position, he is ready to sacrifice himself and accept it: 'Above all, I am most desirous not to seem, as I in truth am not, importunate for any public office whatever. If I were persuaded that a majority of my fellow-citizens desired to place me in their highest executive office, that sense of duty by which I have been ever guided would exact obedience to their will.' [43]

Yet Gallatin, who had every opportunity to study Clay carefully, wrote of him: 'His fault is that he is devoured with ambition and in all his acts never can detach himself and their effect on his popularity from the subject on which he is called to act.' [44] As you follow Clay's correspondence, you can see, as with Webster and Calhoun, the haunting specter of the presidency everywhere. They must have known it, yet they would not admit it, even to themselves. It colored all their views and efforts to some extent, and in Clay's case it is evidently responsible for his inconsistencies, such as they were, and for such trimming as appears in his dealing with the annexation of Texas, which probably lost him the presidency in 1844.

There is over and over again the eager effort, the ardent expectation, and then there is failure, defeat, disappointment, discouragement, disgust. Wise's account of Clay's extraordinary behavior when he lost the nomination to Harrison in 1840 may be exaggerated, but it must have a good deal of basis in fact: 'Such an exhibition we never witnessed before and we pray never again to witness such an ebullition of passion, such a storm of desperation and curses. He rose from his chair, and walking backwards and forwards rapidly, lifting his feet like a horse string-halted in both legs, stamped his steps upon the floor, exclaiming, "My friends are not worth the powder and shot it would take to kill them." He mentioned the names of several, invoking upon them the most horrid imprecations, and then, turning to us, approached rapidly and, stopping before us, with violent gestures and loud voice said, "If there were two Henry

Clays, one of them would make the other President of the United States."' [45]

After such a downfall and the reaction that goes with it, it seems as if there were no hope any more, no use in hoping. One turns back to one's lovely quiet home at Ashland, to one's wife and children, and cries out that retirement and peace are all the joy of life, that one has never longed for anything else. But this plague of ambition cannot be subdued, cannot be obliterated. Strength comes again, hope comes again. There is a little gleam of encouragement from somewhere. Friends urge that duty calls. One would not disregard duty under any circumstances. And at the very next opportunity, one is back in the race, hoping and fighting and sweating and despairing as ardently and pitifully as ever.

Thus, having clearly established Clay's political and human qualities and gifts, we can make, in view of them, a very brief survey of his main efforts in the political field. Many of these efforts failed, in fact most of them failed partially; but they were numerous and varied and almost all of them were high in aim and aspiration, however they proved abortive.

To begin with, Clay was perhaps the main pro-

moter of the War of 1812, and though that war was
not very glorious in some ways, on the whole it
contributed to give the country an international
standing that it had not had before. Another of
Clay's less successful later efforts was in connection
with the sale of the public lands and distribution of
the proceeds among the States. His policy here is
not generally approved, but it had at least a mag-
nanimous as well as a personal intention. Both the
lack of success and the mixture of motives appear
most in the bitter contest with Jackson over the
United States Bank. Here again Clay no doubt
believed he was working for the public welfare.
But Jackson was his worst enemy and hatred and
patriotism make a mixture of strong flavor and
remarkable effectiveness. It is in this connection
that one thinks most of Adams's cruel but penetrating qualification of Clay as 'rancorously bene-
volent.' [46] So much of the world's philanthropy is
not inaptly covered by a similar phrase.

Others of Clay's political schemes and projects
were more purely humanitarian, even when they
were not more successful. He joined Webster in the
effort to procure national sympathy and support
for the struggling Greeks. He toiled long and
zealously to sustain the revolt of South America

from the Spanish tyranny, and if he accomplished little of what he hoped and dreamed, he at least established himself securely in the remembrance of the South American peoples. He worked hard to bring about the development of internal improvements through the whole country and, while the special projects may have come to nothing, the general impetus was not lost. Above all, he devoted himself to the perfection of his 'American System,' in the elaboration of the tariff to protect American industries. He himself was no extreme high-tariff man. He expressly deprecated a desire to turn his country into any such world manufactory as England was. But he believed in developing American industry at least in proportion to American needs, and his speeches and arguments have served two or three generations of eager followers since his time.

Unquestionably Clay's supreme political achievements may be best summed up in the word 'compromise.' His contemporaries called him 'The Great Pacificator.' The phrase has been disputed on the ground that many of the compromises he pushed did not originate with him; but in the spirit of compromise and the full appreciation of the significance of it he was unrivaled.

HENRY CLAY

Compromise was characteristic of him and embodied the humanness which we have all along emphasized as so essential in his heart. It was not weakness, it was not timidity. No one was more daring in asserting the truths of which he was convinced, or more positive in his own view where he had deliberately adopted it, though it was sometimes alleged, not altogether unjustly, that he was more ardent in discovering political principles and in establishing them than in persisting with them. But the basis of his idea of compromise was simply human understanding and sympathy, the intense desire to enter into the point of view of others and to make it your own, so far as possible. All arguments were dubious. All human reasoning was fallible. At least you should recognize that others meant well, that they were honest, earnest, patriotic in intention, as you were. If you started on this basis, some method of adjustment, of mutual comprehension and agreement, might surely be discovered. A forthright sticking to one's own opinions might push the world forward by leaps and jerks; but to keep it in stable equilibrium, to manage it practically, concession and compromise were absolutely indispensable. The Constitution of the United States was the grand example of compromise, and it was the principle of compromise that originally made that Constitution possible and made it endure. No finer statement of the theory can be found than that uttered by Clay in his very last years: 'I go for honorable compromise wherever it can be made. Life itself is but a compromise between death and life, the struggle continuing throughout our whole existence, until the great destroyer finally triumphs. All legislation, all government, all society is founded upon the principle of mutual concession, politeness, comity, courtesy; upon these everything is based. I bow to you to-day because you bow to me. . . . Let him who elevates himself above humanity, above its weaknesses, its infirmities, its wants, its necessities, say, if he pleases, I never will compromise, but let no one who is not above the frailties of our common nature disdain compromise.' [47]

The first of Clay's great efforts at compromise was the Missouri Compromise of 1820, which was initiated by others, but carried through largely by his persistent urgency and untiring zeal. It fixed, of course, in regard to slavery generally, much the view held by Clay himself, and that was merely a compromise between general humanitarian hatred in the abstract and the practical accommodation of habit and convenience. Then, in 1832, there was the tariff compromise, which by giving up or modifying Clay's extreme principles, averted the threat of Nullification for the time, though this agreement Clay is said to have later regretted. And the supreme performance in this line was the great Slavery Compromise of 1850, which was finally carried through more by the influence of Clay and Webster combined than by anything else. Here again there has been plenty of criticism, but the preponderant verdict at present seems to be that, halting and imperfect as the compromise was, it saved the Union by postponing the struggle until the growing power of the North got the immense development of the West behind it.

But, whatever judgment may be passed upon these compromises in their practical working, it must be admitted that in them and in all the other phases of his political life Clay was earnestly, ardently patriotic. Indeed, in everything he was frank, direct, sincere. Such social charm as his is sometimes associated with duplicity, and he was accused of this, as of many other human frailties. But the truth is, he had a candid, outspoken, genuine soul. Over and over again he asserts his sincerity, and it is impossible not to believe him.

At the same time, an ordinary person, who does not make a business of public life, is occasionally somewhat astonished by the tremendous solemnity with which Clay makes this assertion. Take one passage among many: 'I can say, and in the presence of my God and of this assembled multitude I will say, that I have honestly and faithfully served my country; that I have never wronged it; and that, however unprepared I lament that I am to appear in the Divine presence on other accounts, I invoke the stern justice of his judgment on my public conduct, without the smallest apprehension of his displeasure.' [48] I should not dare to offer such a challenge with regard to any phase of my life or conduct for the existence of a single day. Yet Clay flings it in the face of Almighty God for thirty years. Of such stuff the great rulers of the world are made.

IV

Finally, we may conclude with some larger applications of Clay's thorough and most winning humanness. He was essentially democratic. This does not mean that he cultivated the cheap arts of the demagogue. He did not slap Tom, Dick, and Harry on the back at street corners, or tell uproarious stories in bar-rooms. His personal bearing in public and in private was always dignified. But, like Lincoln, he believed in the mass of the people, their political honesty and sanity. He had not a trace of the profound mistrust which affects so many wise men to-day, and which is the mere reaction from the too great hopes and enthusiasms of a century ago. Clay believed in the common man because he loved him and felt himself to be essentially like him. At the beginning of his career he proclaimed: 'I have no commiseration for princes. My sympathies are reserved for the great mass of mankind.' [49] And the rhetoric in this, as in so many others of his utterances, is softened and sweetened by the feeling behind it. As one who knew him well expressed it: 'His sympathies were as wide as human nature and his manner was but the easy and natural expression of this sympathy. He recognized a certain dignity in every human soul which excited his respect and consideration.' [50]

And Clay was ever a passionate and hopeful supporter of the American Union. He knew the value of the State tradition and said the right word for it at the right time. But he believed that the Union was an absolute necessity for all the States and for the future of mankind and he held those who were disloyal to it to be traitors. As Lincoln said of him: 'Feeling as he did, and as the truth surely is, that the world's best hope depends on the continued union of these States, he was ever jealous of and watchful for whatever might have the slightest tendency to separate them.' [51] Or, as Clay expressed it, with a passionate ardor quite worthy of Lincoln himself: 'If any one desires to know the leading and paramount object of my public life, the preservation of this Union will furnish him the key.' [52] It cannot be doubted that Clay's influence went far toward preserving the Union in the generation that followed his.

Moreover, Clay was essentially, constructively, triumphantly American. It would be perhaps unjust to say that he was more so than Webster. But Webster's Americanism was of the head, Clay's of the heart. Webster's America was largely English. Clay's America was the America of the future, however destiny might shape it. The aim of Webster was to affirm, to maintain, to strengthen the American Union on the fruitful basis of its original design. The effort of Calhoun was to preserve it in its elementary framework, with the alternative of ruin, if one joint of the ancient structure, as he saw it, was shaken or imperiled. The impetuous impulse of Clay was to let the youth, the vigor, the

creative spirit of triumphant America sweep in
untrammeled activity whithersoever it would, secure that a beneficent Providence would guide it
in the future as it had done in the past.

And in all these various phases Clay embodied
the spirit of the West. Webster was the type of the
Eastern tradition, Calhoun of the Southern. But
the splendid, new, dynamic energy of the developing Western country found its true representative
in Henry Clay. Jackson perhaps had more rough,
aggressive, popular democracy. But Clay's was the
Western good-humor and good-nature, its large
cordiality, its breezy friendliness and readiness to
grasp and understand. Clay's was its nervous vigor,
its all-attempting courage, its undying enthusiasm.
It was the West of Henry Clay that gave us food,
that gave us fresh air, that gave us hope, and that
gave us Clay's inheritor in many respects, the child
of his own Kentucky, the supreme embodiment of
the Western spirit, the savior of the Union, Abraham Lincoln.

III
JOHN CALDWELL CALHOUN

CHRONOLOGY

Jоhn Caldwell Calhoun

Born, September 12, 1782, at Abbeville, South Carolina.

Graduated, Yale, 1804.

Elected to House of Representatives, 1810.

Married Floride Calhoun, January 8, 1811.

Secretary of War, 1817–1825.

Vice-President, 1825–1832.

Active for Nullification, 1832.

Senator, 1833–1843.

Senator, 1845–1850.

Last words in Senate, March 13, 1850.

Died, March 31, 1850.

JOHN C. CALHOUN

JOHN CALDWELL CALHOUN

I

CALHOUN seems to have impressed his contemporaries mainly as a thinking machine. So shrewd an observer as Harriet Martineau spoke of him as 'the càst-iron man, who looks as if he had never been born.' [1] And Mrs. Jefferson Davis said that he always appeared to her 'a moral and mental abstraction.' [2] We shall look later for the flaws in this intellectual solidity, the breaking of human emotion and passion and weakness into the clear, cold, logical fabric which this Scotch-Irish reasoner would have liked to maintain. But even in his more ardent youth he lived in an atmosphere of speculation and argument, and as his physical arteries hardened, his spiritual arteries also hardened in a grim rigidness of systematic theory: the world must be twisted and distorted into the high ideal mould he set for it, or it must break and fall in pieces, as his world did in the generation that followed him.

John Caldwell Calhoun was born in Abbeville, South Carolina, in 1782, of that sturdy Scotch-

Irish stock which brought so much vigor to the Southern United States. His father died when John was thirteen years old, and the boy was delicate in health and had his early education largely out of doors. Later his family decided that something might be made of him and sent him to Dr. Waddell's preparatory school and to Yale, where he was graduated in 1804. He went afterwards to a law school in Litchfield, Connecticut, and then for a time practiced law in his native State. He entered the House of Representatives in 1811, and took an active part with Clay in forcing Madison into the war with England. Calhoun also advocated other measures of a decidedly national character. From 1817 till 1825 he was Monroe's Secretary of War and then until 1832 Vice-President. During all these years he was more or less thought of for the presidency, but his quarrel with Jackson disposed of the ambition for the time. He then turned more and more to the South, championed South Carolina in the tariff-nullification controversy, and opposed Jackson on various issues. In 1844–45, as Tyler's Secretary of State, he was largely instrumental in the annexation of Texas, but he opposed the Mexican War. His later thoughts and hopes were all given to the welfare of the South, and he was distinctly hostile to the Compromise of Webster and Clay, but died in the spring of 1850, before that Compromise went into effect. Calhoun married his cousin Floride Calhoun, in 1811, had a large family of children, and lived his home life entirely on his great estates in South Carolina. Through all this long life the acute, penetrating, metaphysical Scotch intellect predominated, and it is worth while to begin with the training of that intellect and its most important activity in political affairs.

The effects of late education are manifest in Calhoun. His mind had taken its natural mould and bent, before outside mental discipline was extensively applied. One curious result of this is the incorrect spelling which appears in even his later correspondence. When he reached Yale, he learned with extreme rapidity and energy, and he exercised his logical disposition in argument with the violent Federalism of the head of the College, Timothy Dwight, who is said to have predicted that the young man would some day be President. One of his law teachers at Litchfield, Gould, had a remarkable faculty of clear, logical exposition, and it is possible that this may have accentuated Calhoun's natural tendencies to a considerable degree.

It is notable that Calhoun was never a general reader at any time in his life. What he read he remembered and made part of his own independent thinking, but his books, from a very early age, were mainly of an historical and political nature. He read the Greek and Roman political writers, especially Aristotle, whom he much recommended to young men. He read also the thinkers of the eighteenth century, Locke and Burke, and perhaps the French to some extent. His own peculiar ideas were much influenced by his American predecessors, Jefferson and Paine, the writers of 'The Federalist,' and most of all John Taylor of Caroline, who attacked the encroachment of the Federal Government with such bitterness in the early years of the century.

But Calhoun's chief school was evidently solitary thought, and his mind and his whole career show the benefits and the defects of such a training. His father early interested him in politics, and in the long, lonely days on the South Carolina farm, the boy formed the habit of thinking things out hard and steadily for himself. All his life, as his biographer says, 'he spent a great deal of time in solitary thought.'³ As in all such cases, what he got was his own, and he held to it with superb tenacity, but he was too much inclined to force it upon others, and to pay little heed to what others might have to offer him.

Calhoun's first years in the House of Representatives were ardently national, and much of his later ingenuity was given to trying to explain this away, quite unnecessarily. He favored the establishment of the Bank. He favored the high tariff and the protection of manufactures. He favored internal improvements, and this latter interest stuck by him all his life, so that even in 1845 he presided over the Memphis Convention for the development of the Mississippi Valley. In what remains of his earlier speeches on these topics the general mental characteristics are evident, the clear, direct, logical insistence, the assumption that all you need do to lead men is to convince them. There is still something of youth in the form, an occasional touch of rhetoric which is later got rid of. But Calhoun's oratory, in youth and age, appealed to the minds of men rather than to their hearts. His speech was tense, crowded, rugged, hard to grasp and to hold. His manner was dignified and commanding, and his eyes, which are emphasized, like those of Clay and Webster, had an enthralling, magnetic power. But Mrs. Davis says that 'his voice was not musical;

it was the voice of a professor of mathematics, and suited his didactic discourse admirably.' 4

During the years of his Secretaryship of War and Vice-Presidency, from 1817 to 1832, Calhoun was politically quiescent, except for administrative detail. All this time he was more or less tantalized by aspiration to the presidency and he had good hopes of obtaining it through Jackson. Then there came the scandal of Mrs. Eaton, who was favored by Jackson and snubbed by Mrs. Calhoun and the ladies of the Cabinet. Jackson was further embittered by discovering that Calhoun, who he thought had stood by him at the time of his high-handed action in Florida in 1818, had really been critical and adverse. After this, Jackson hated Calhoun almost as ardently as he hated Clay, and Calhoun's presidential prospects again grew dim. From that time on he became more and more sectional. Personal disappointment perhaps entered in, but it may justly be assumed that he felt more and more the peril and the isolation of the South, and the keen intelligence which had begun by working so eagerly for national interests now turned to asserting and maintaining the cause of a special group. In this regard too much of Calhoun's strength was spent upon the charge of inconsistency. In his saner moods he treated the matter with common sense: 'true consistency, that of the prudent and the wise, is to act in conformity with circumstances, and not to act always the same way under a change of circumstances.' [5] But it is an excellent remark of Von Holst that each of the three great rivals, Clay, Webster, and Calhoun, expended much energy in defending his own consistency and attacking that of the others; 'each of them was perfectly successful as to the latter task, and, in spite of infinite ingenuity and eloquence, sadly failed as to the former.'

Calhoun's intense sectional activity showed itself in various aspects, though it must be remembered that he himself denied that it was wholly sectional and insisted that he would fight for the North, when it was oppressed, just as much as for the South. He was strongly opposed to Clay's high protective tariff, and when South Carolina was ready to resist by force, he was one of the most powerful advocates of the ingenious doctrine of Nullification, by which a sovereign State was justified in refusing to obey a Federal law which it held to be incompatible with the Constitution. Calhoun told Mrs. Maury that he could wish to have Nullification written on his tombstone. [7] But he was referring not so much to action in a particular case as to what seemed to him the essential assertion of a governmental principle.

Again, Calhoun opposed the tendency of the North in financial matters. He certainly thought long on such points and to one not well versed in them it would seem acutely. He disbelieved in the Bank because of its centralizing tendency: but it is especially interesting to see him anticipating modern radicalism in the intense dread and distrust of the money power in governmental dealings. 'Property,' he says, 'is in its nature timid, and seeks protection, and nothing is more gratifying to Government than to become a protector.'[8] Hence he deduces and shows a horror of Wall Street that would suit the most violent agitator of to-day: 'Wall Street (the head and centre, in our country, of the great moneyed, bank, stock, and paper interest, domestic and foreign) is in the ascendant in the councils of the Union. Every measure is controlled by it, and at its pleasure; — banks, brokers, and stock-jobbers sway everything.'[9] To be sure, the protest would be somewhat more effective, if Calhoun himself had not represented a form of capitalism as narrow and aristocratic as any industrialism of the North.

JOHN CALDWELL CALHOUN

For, even more than in the tariff and in finance, he was absorbed and engrossed in protecting and maintaining the institution of slavery. In the early days of the Republic the statesmen of the South disliked slaveholding and would gladly have got rid of it. Clay hated it, though he found it comfortable to live with. Calhoun and his followers, like Jefferson Davis, apologized for it radically; more than that defended it, gloried in it. Calhoun's most definite political act was the annexation of Texas, which he accomplished as Tyler's Secretary of State in 1845; and to his death he proclaimed with increasing vehemence that in the Southern States slavery, instead of being an evil, was 'a good — a positive good,' [10] and that for all parties concerned. This aggressive attitude, resulting largely from changed agricultural conditions, necessarily increased the bitterness on both sides, and in the end went far to precipitate a perhaps inevitable conflict.

Closely bound up with these sectional interests in Calhoun's case was his deeper and broader attitude toward the whole question of the Constitution and State Rights. He professed at all times to be and no doubt was a lover of the Union, but it was the Union as he conceived it, not transformed

97

or disfigured by encroaching Federalism, but the pure ideal of the Fathers. That there ever was any pure ideal of the Fathers may well be questioned, and impartial analysis will probably in the end regard the Constitution as an elaborate and ingenious compromise, cunningly devised to serve its purpose, but capable, like most compromises, of being tortured into any interpretation that would serve the ends of those who wished to argue about it. At any rate, Calhoun, like many others before and after him, under pretense of the most dignified and ardent conservatism, read the poor instrument in his own fashion, until he made it yield conclusions which would have been as distasteful to some of its framers as they would have been acceptable to others. And all the time it must be remembered that Calhoun's father had fought the Constitution, because he claimed it would draw power and dignity from the States.

Nor was Calhoun's political thinking confined to the technical puzzles of the Constitution. In breadth and vigor of general theorizing he far surpassed Clay, and, as it seems to me, decidedly even Webster. Professor Channing says, 'His "Disquisition on Government" is one of the most memorable books on politics that this country has yet

produced.' " The distrust of extreme democracy
which has become so apparent of late years is very
marked in Calhoun, and he complains bitterly of
the despotism of the numerical majority. He also
anticipates modern thinking in the effort to establish minority representation. He does indeed recognize what seems to some of us the most valid check
upon majority tyranny, that is, the balance of
power in the hands of the moderate, who can swing
the majority to one side or the other, but he justly
insists that this ceases to be effective when the
majority becomes mainly sectional, as was the case
in his day. To control this preponderance of mere
number, he devised an ingenious theory of what he
called 'concurrent majorities,' by which all the
interests in the community would be represented
and protected, and his idea of Nullification was
that it embodied this notion of a concurrent majority acting through the States. To many of us, however, the extreme reasoning of the two incomplete
treatises, to which he devoted his later years, must
seem somewhat fantastic, as in his plan to sub-
stitute for the single president two consuls, one
elected by the North and the other by the South,
who should share the executive functions between
them.

AS GOD MADE THEM

What above all interests me in the political reasoning of Calhoun is to discover whether he has any sense of the terrible danger and difficulty of the reasoning process, so abstractly and tyrannously pursued. Some slight personal attempt to solve the problems of the universe, and a considerable observation of the attempts of others, have impressed me chiefly with the snares, pitfalls, and quagmires into which the untrammeled indulgence of the intellect is apt to lead, and I ask myself how far Calhoun was aware of these and how far he allowed for them. The answer appears to be, very little. Occasionally there is an apologetic suggestion of possible error, an intimation that others may be right, but such gleams are rare.

Instead, there is an unfailing insistence that reason must prevail, that it is the one infallible guide in human affairs, and that John C. Calhoun, from long experience and natural acumen, reasons correctly: it is only for others to accept and submit. I cannot be mistaken, my conclusions follow my premises, as the night the day: that is the usual tone. And such sheer confidence in one's own intellectual processes begets, as it always must, a sheer confidence in one's self, not a shallow, pretentious vanity, but a calm, secure certainty that one is working in unison with the order of the world, and that those who differ are misled by their own folly or by something worse. Calhoun's latest, sympathetic, and also on the whole judicious biographer, Mr. Meigs, insists that the campaign biography of his hero, published in 1845, is mainly autobiographic. This I am reluctant to allow; for it is hard to conceive that any self-respecting man could indulge in such continuous and fatuous self-laudation. But Calhoun's own indisputable expressions of the extreme self-confidence are quite enough, are really overwhelming. Those who find the past made up chiefly of mistakes and regrets will gasp over the quiet satisfaction of a man who could write: 'In looking back, I see nothing to regret, and little to correct.' [12] Those who feel that they err and falter and stumble at every step can only wonder at the splendid assurance which finds the march of the universe behind it: 'Whether it be too great confidence in my own opinion I cannot say, but what I think I see, I see with so much apparent clearness as not to leave me a choice to pursue any other course, which has always given me the impression that I acted with the force of destiny.' [13]

AS GOD MADE THEM

II

As we have thus seen how completely Calhoun was dominated by the intellect in political matters, it is interesting to watch the working of his intellect in other sides and phases of life.

Sometimes the pure thinker goes astray in practical affairs, carries his head so high in the clouds that he trips over obstacles which a more limited vision would deal with clearly. This was by no means the case with Calhoun. He had Scotch blood in him, and Scotch habit: this made him think hard, but it also made him keenly alive to practical realities.

He was an excellent man of business. This is obvious and undeniable in public affairs. As an administrator, he managed the War Department with distinguished success. He himself tells us so, if he is really responsible for the so-called autobiography of 1845, and though the critical John Quincy Adams criticizes, as always, other testimony is too favorable and even enthusiastic to be disputed. The Secretary was an energetic and systematic organizer. He applied his intelligence and vision in reforms that were sorely needed and were far-reaching in their effect. Also, what one would much less look for, he was ready to consider the

suggestions of others, and to profit by them, and
what one would look for least of all, he made himself exceedingly popular, and was liked and praised
by the army officers, even while he was introducing
new methods which might have been expected to
agitate and irritate.

There was the same solid good sense in the man's
private concerns. The keen, systematic intelligence
systematized and ordered the conduct of daily life.
When he was at home on his plantation, he lived
by the clock, going and coming according to an
established routine, and the same system appears
to have been introduced into all his affairs. In
money matters he was an excellent manager,
shrewd and thrifty, yet by no means niggardly or
grasping. Indeed, he disclaimed the love of money,
and especially the commercial forms of making it,
which he rejected with horror: 'I would not be rich
in America; for the care of money would distract
my mind from more important concerns.' [14] Above
all, he was strictly, scrupulously honest as to
the dangerous mixture of money and politics. At
one time he endeavored to interest some Northern capitalists in a business undertaking. They responded, but he imagined that the response was
less from business interest than from personal re-

gard for him, and he instantly refused to take the money: 'When I wrote you, I had supposed that a loan might be effected from the state of the money market on terms mutually advantageous. It was only on that supposition that I could make the offer, or accept the loan.' [15] This shows a disposition in such matters very different from that of Daniel Webster.

Calhoun's instinct for systematic, practical management appears in his handling of his great plantation, Fort Hill. To begin with, he loved it. It meant home to him, and the days in Washington, however exciting, were exile. In early years he writes: 'You will see by this letter that my passion for farming is not abated. In fact, I consider my absence from my farm among my greatest sacrifices.' [16] And the fondness grew as dissatisfaction with public affairs increased. It must be admitted that, owing to financial conditions and difficulties, which pressed hard upon so many planters besides himself, the farm was not a great money-maker. 'Account books of Calhoun's own estate reveal a moving story of a losing venture,' says Mr. Beard.[17] But this was not from lack of thought, or care, or assiduous attention on Calhoun's part, and a neighbor, who knew the circumstances well,

writes that the farmer-statesman aimed directly at
results and attained these 'with a practical sagac-
ity which I had not expected in a mind so intensely
theoretical.' [18]

We are not told so much as we could wish about
Calhoun's management of his slaves, but it is evident that the large and theoretical conception of
things entered in here also, and further the perfect
satisfaction with his own methods and his own attitude. When an anxious Northern admirer wrote
to ask about some charges of harshness and cruelty,
Calhoun replied: 'My character as a master is, I
trust, as unimpeachable, as I hope it is in all the
other relations of life. I regard my relation to those
who belong to me in the double aspect of master
and guardian, and am as careful to discharge the
duties appertaining to each, as I am those which ap-
pertain to the numerous other relations in which
I am placed.' [19] A curious and vivid picture of the
working of this arbitrary and unquestioned theoretical authority and satisfaction is given in Mrs.
Maury's account of what she observed during her
visit: 'His gracious, princely nature, accustomed
to give commands without appeal, is equally accustomed to receiving submission without reserve;
hence his gentleness, hence his indulgence, hence

his compassion: no vulgar upstart display of authority is traced in his intercourse with those who own him for their lord . . . he is served with the perfect love that casteth out fear.' [20] I wonder.

If we turn to the working of Calhoun's intellect in more general abstract fields, the story is somewhat different. Whenever there was call for the application of acute, penetrating analysis in detail, he was always ready. That singular document which Mr. Meigs calls an autobiography tells us: 'To these advantages he adds another, which constitutes perhaps his highest quality as a statesman. It is the faculty of considering circumstances in their combinations and of determining their relative power in propelling events. To analyze this combination, or "juncture" (as he sometimes calls it), and to determine the result of all these forces is, in his opinion, the highest and rarest faculty of a statesman.' [21]

But when it comes to the larger use of reason in other fields than politics, or the immediate consideration of character, there seems to be little sign of it. It is indeed said that Calhoun took a great interest in science and contributed toward scientific research. It is certain that he could talk interestingly on a surprising variety of subjects, and an

admiring lady says: 'I have never been more convinced of Mr. Calhoun's genius than to-day while
he talked to us of a flower.' [22] But no such scientific
interest appears in the vast correspondence, nothing of Jefferson's ever-active curiosity about
new thoughts and new discoveries.

Nor does Calhoun show any more energetic
ardor in philosophical thought, though one might
suppose that his quality of intellect would have led
naturally in this direction. He read the Greek and
the English and French philosophers when they
dealt with the political nature of man, but larger
consideration of man's origin and destiny seemed
to be beyond his range.

The same is true of religion. Calhoun was
brought up in the strictest Scotch orthodoxy.
Though he was never inclined to discuss such matters, it is said that in later years he leaned toward
freer theological views. But he expressed great
reverence for the Bible, especially when it could be
used as an argument for slavery, and the Calvinistic
attitude of stern repression and struggle clung to
him always: 'I hold the duties of life to be greater
than life itself, and that in performing them man-
fully, even against hope, our labor is not lost, but
will be productive of good in after times. Indeed

I regard this life very much as a struggle against evil, and that to him who acts on proper principle, *the reward is in the struggle more than in victory itself*, although that greatly enhances it.' [23] The practical application of the same attitude appears admirably in Mrs. Chesnut's story of the man who sought Calhoun's ample and generous Southern hospitality: 'He allowed everybody to stay all night who chose to stop at his house. An ill-mannered person on one occasion refused to attend family prayers. Mr. Calhoun said to the servant, "Saddle the man's horse and let him go." From the traveler Calhoun would take no excuse for the "Deity offended."' [24]

From these larger considerations I deduce that Calhoun's intellect, acute and active as it was, did not instinctively go to the very bottom of things. Even in political thinking, when it comes to fundamentals, it seems to me that he is a little apt to assume and take on trust. It is the working of a mind that has been self-educated, without stern academic discipline, and is proud of it. Again, I do not feel that he has what I call the passion of thinking. His reason is always busy, always muscularly agitated. But he is not torn by that madness of doubt and question which drove Lucretius, for example, to wrench and strain at the roots of life in the vain effort to make them yield up all their mystery. Calhoun is too happily secure in every step of his reasoning processes to feel the agony of doubt, and without such agony I do not believe that any one reaches the profoundest depths of wisdom. At the same time there is no disputing that Calhoun was essentially an intellectualist. For him the whole surface of life was netted over with the tenuous web of argumentative speculation, and again and again one feels with him the force of Leopardi's remark, that 'there is nothing more unphilosophical than the effort to make the whole of life philosophical.' [25]

III

It is a fascinating study to search for breaks and flaws in the systematic, steely completeness of Calhoun's intellectual armor, and his extensive correspondence is a great help in this. His communication with his friends is frank, direct, self-revealing, far more so than the letters of Clay, or of Webster, or even of Jefferson. Yet it must be confessed that the evidences of emotional experience are not very abundant. Calhoun had a nervous and highly sensitive organization, but in general it was well under control. There are occasional references to this sensibility, as when, on receiving the pledge of Webster's assistance in a difficult undertaking, Calhoun 'burst into tears.' [26] And there are frequent indications of melancholy and even of a pessimistic tendency, so that one asks one's self if extreme intellectualism is not apt to carry such a tendency with it, till one remembers that Emerson's intense mental activity produced an optimism far more positive and constant. Calhoun at times, indeed, insists upon his cheerful view of things and speaks of 'my non-despairing disposition,' [27] but the general drift toward a dismal outlook is too evident. He knew what was right and what ought to be done, but the mass of men were blind and stupid, and such blindness and stupidity must bring disaster.

In more general manifestations of emotional life the barrenness is even more marked. Æsthetic interest is extraordinarily wanting. Even Nature, though there are some charming hints of appreciation, is treated more as a cotton producer than as a thing of beauty. The record for painting and music is as utterly blank as with Clay and Webster, and that for literature far more so. Calhoun is said to have made one attempt at poetry, which began with 'Whereas': he made no more. He almost never quotes the poets, shows no sign that they existed.

He does, indeed, repeat verses on one occasion to a lady at dinner, but the instance is so unusual as to demand special comment.[28] Late in life he was found turning over the pages of a novel at the request of a lady, and he remarked that it was the first book of the kind he had ever read. [29] Yet he undertook to be a leader of men!

The same lack of intense experience appears in religious matters. Of course those who feel most in this line often say least. Still with Calhoun, one wonders, or, no, one does not wonder very much. No doubt he prayed faithfully: I should like to know how and what he prayed, certainly not that God would enable him to see the right, for he saw it anyway. As to public worship, he highly approved of it, and why? because 'shaking hands with your neighbor at the church-door, asking after his family, even remarking that it is a pleasant day — these all have a wonderful power in binding men together.' [30] I would not imply that Calhoun was less subject to emotion than many men, only that his special intellectual bent overrode and perhaps in the end stunted other activities and interests.

With the more specially human relations it is something the same; yet here it must be insisted and emphasized that Calhoun had a singular charm.

III

As to love, there is no record of any other woman than his wife, early or late. If he looked at others in his youth, it is not mentioned. His attachment for his wife was profound and lasting, and she deserved it. His biographer even insists that his wooing brought out the romantic side of his nature. Perhaps this is a little strong, though the epistolary style of a hundred years ago was always somewhat formal and frigid and the lover's early ardor has undeniable charm: 'I am not much given to enthusiasm, nor to anticipate future happiness. But, I cannot now refrain my hopes of joy. On my part, I feel the anxious solicitude for the happiness of one to me dearer than all others.' [31] Yet, to my thinking, the intellectualist peers through everywhere. He is most careful to bring forward elaborate arguments for not being willing to make any settlement on the young lady. [32] The lurking analysis of curious reason will intrude itself: 'Should I always remain with my present feeling, which I trust in God I may.' [33] And most characteristic of all is the following brief touch: 'After a careful examination, I find none but those qualities in her character, which are suited to me.' [34]

Calhoun had nine children. He was devoted to them and he was more fortunate in keeping them than either Webster or Clay. He was fond of little children and was considerate and tender with them, and one who visited in his household says that 'he is adored in his family, and his manners, at all times agreeable, at home are captivating.' [35] Yet again I find the man written all over in the consolation that he offered to his wife on the loss of a child: 'I tell her it is the lot of humanity; that almost all parents have suffered equal calamity; that Providence may have intended it in kindness to her and ourselves, as no one can say what, had she lived, would have been her condition; ... and above all we have the consolation to know that she is far more happy than she could be here with us.' [36] And he is amazed to find that this seems to grieve her the more. Especially, I am impressed by the barely, tragically appropriate circumstances of his solitary death in Washington. 'He had resolutely forbidden that his wife should be sent for, ... not wishing that she should be put to inconvenience. ... Crallé was struck with the absence of any signs of feminine attention in the sick-chamber. On the narrow mantelpiece was a lump of cold boiled rice, a glass of water, some dried prunes, and a feeble tallow candle. As the night wore on, the noise of merrymaking in other parts of the house sometimes pene-

trated the sick-room, and occasionally some one
would look in to ask if he still lived.' [37] Thus that
bright, steady torch of reason, which had burned
so long, tranquilly flickered out.

It is probable that Calhoun's slaves were attached to him, though evidence on this head is
naturally hard to procure. Adam, his father's first
acquisition, was a sort of factotum in the family,
and Adam's son was John's intimate workfellow
and playfellow. Mrs. Maury, who to be sure is
inclined to eulogy, says: 'He watches his slaves in
their sickness, provides for their hunger, thirst, and
age; protects their wives and nourishes their children.' [38] All of which was of course good business
as well as philanthropy. I do not know whether the
sole recorded instance of punishment, the distasteful affair of Aleck, exhibits temper or theory, but I
suspect that a bitter and resentful temper enters
into it. Aleck, a house servant, had offended his
mistress, been threatened with a whipping, and
run away. Calhoun writes to his brother-in-law to
catch him and have him 'severely whipped.' When
he is caught, the request is repeated: 'He ran away
for no other cause but to avoid a correction for
some misconduct, and as I am desirous to prevent
a repetition, I wish you to have him lodged in jail

for one week, to be fed on bread and water, and to employ some one for me to give him thirty lashes, well laid on, at the end of the time.' [39]

When we come to more general human relations and interests, Calhoun makes no great showing. He did not seek people because he did not need people. Ordinary social diversions and amusements did not attract him. In his younger days he liked the solitary sports, hunting and fishing: they had practical value. But the games that bring men together were not in his line. He had never robust health, took little interest in what he ate, and none in what he drank. He had always vigor enough to do what he considered his duty, but he had no excess of vigor for late hours or irregular living. It is amusing to see the awe with which Webster, in his eulogy, speaks of this utter indifference to the diversions that meant so much to him: 'I have known no man who wasted less of life in what is called recreation, or employed less of it in any pursuits not immediately connected with the discharge of his duty.' [40]

Of intimate personal friendship there is little sign in Calhoun's career. One of his closest relations, outside his immediate family, was with his mother-in-law, to whom he became deeply attached before his marriage, and to whom he wrote self-revealing and confidential letters. His ideals of friendship were high — and theoretical. Everything but consideration for duty might be disregarded for those one loved: 'I cheerfully yield my own claims to such consideration, and no friend can ask me to go further. I ask no sacrifice of any friend, which I would not cheerfully make myself. Indeed, I would much rather make the sacrifice than ask a friend to make it.' [41] But in practical life he does not seem to have found many with whom he shared his inmost heart, if he had one to share.

General social occasions he avoided if he could. He says of Washington, in his early years: 'This place is quite gay during the session; but I do not participate in it much myself. You know I never had much inclination to such enjoyment.' [42] The inclination did not increase with age. And in his social efforts the curious intellectualism intrudes, as everywhere else. 'I always endeavor to make the place I reside in agreeable; from a conviction that it is necessary to every other enjoyment.' [43] Yet in spite of this unsocial habit, he was amply hospitable always, and the universal testimony is that visitors found him delightful. Clay, who did not love him, said, 'he is a most captivating man.' [44] He was frank, simple, absolutely genuine at all times. Especially he was attractive to the young, taking the greatest pains to talk with them as naturally and whole-heartedly as he did to their elders. There are numerous and most attractive descriptions of this peculiar social charm. Mrs. Davis, who had an energetic, assertive personality of her own, speaks feelingly of his fascination, and above all of the magnetic power of his eyes.[45] Oliver Dyer, who studied Washington political life very carefully, and arrived with every prejudice against Calhoun, was completely converted, and after first considering him the embodiment of Milton's Satan, came to this very decided eulogy: 'He was inexpressibly urbane, refined, gentle, winning; and yet he was strong and thoroughly manly, with an elegance and engaging invincibleness. I admired Benton; I admired Clay still more; I admired Webster, on the intellectual side, most of all; but I loved Calhoun.' [46]

As to the quality of Calhoun's conversation, accounts differ somewhat. There is no question as to the ample abundance of it. But many people found it self-engrossed and wearisome. One neighbor of some importance and distinction remarked: 'I hate a man who makes me think so much. For the last three hours I have been on the stretch, trying to follow him through heaven and earth. I feel wearied with the effort; and I hate a man who makes me feel my own inferiority.' [47] On the other hand, Mrs. Davis felt that his gentleness and sympathy invited confidence to an unusual extent. And Dyer is even more enthusiastic, commending the voice, which is not commonly commended: 'He talked on the most abstruse subjects with the guileless simplicity of a prattling child. His ideas were so clear and his language so plain that he made a path of light through any subject he discussed.' [48] This latter quality, of a singular direct, revealing frankness, is emphasized by every one, and doubtless accounted largely for the charm. At any rate, it is evident that it was worth while to go a long way to hear Calhoun talk.

Humor seems to have been hopelessly lacking in Calhoun's make-up, and his deficiency in this regard is beyond that of even most statesmen. He rarely made, or enjoyed, or invited a jest of any kind. Nothing more clearly marks the extreme, intense intellectualism that was predominant in him.

On the negative side of social life, that of difficulties and quarrels, it seems to me that, without exaggerating, one easily detects again the intellectual attitude. In one sense it may be said that Calhoun did not have enemies, would not allow himself to have them. But he was right, therefore his opponents were wrong, and if they were wrong, it was likely that some moral slant or turpitude entered in. In this respect Calhoun is too sadly inclined to attribute base motives, almost as much so as John Quincy Adams, who indeed attributed them to Calhoun himself in later years, though earlier inclined to commend him highly.

Calhoun's bitterest quarrel was with Andrew Jackson, and this kept cropping up in phase after phase. The initiative in the matter, at least as regards the first outbreak, lay with Jackson; but Calhoun had given him excuse in letting him suppose that he had been friendly to him in the Florida affair, whereas he had been quite the reverse. Jackson kept up the feud with all his usual ferocity, and Calhoun with steady, critical persistence and unyielding determination. They were as different in temper as two men could be, Jackson quick, impulsive, instinctive, often indiscreet, Calhoun cool, calculating, deliberate. They were both Scotch, and a Scotch quarrel is apt to last long, but in his later years Calhoun spoke of his great adversary with esteem and admiration.

AS GOD MADE THEM

The quarrel with Jackson lets us see into the greatest of all the flaws in Calhoun's intellectual equipment, the intense ambition for the presidency, which haunted him as it did Clay and Webster. He of course repeatedly disclaimed this ambition, just as they did: he was animated only by the sense of public duty and the feeling that he could save the country. It is at any rate clear that no conscious motives affected him except the highest. Yet he liked to be a leader, even though he had not Clay's magnetic gift of leadership. He liked to feel that the country looked up to him, that 'when Calhoun took snuff, South Carolina sneezed,' and the eager thirst for the greatest honor American political life had to give appears on page after page of the vast correspondence. Failure, disappointment, might check it for the moment. Then some spark of sympathy or hope would set it blazing as ardently as ever. His contemporaries were apt to insinuate that ambition ran away with him, just as he said the same thing of them. Adams and many others accused him of sacrificing honesty and loyalty to the one great aspiration. This is unfair and untrue. But he did want to be President, and here also his logical habit was a help and a spur to him. He was convinced, by irrefragable arguments, that he was the best man to govern the country, and if that was so, duty obliged him to welcome any opportunity that came. There can be no more curious psychological revelation of the working of complicated motives than the numerous passages in which he displays and dissects this state of mind, as, for example, in 1831: 'If the country wants an individual to carry on the sectional conflicts, I am not their man. I would not advance myself by sacrificing its true interests; but if they look to the higher considerations of peace, harmony, and liberty, it would be the proudest incident of my life to be instrumental in promoting these great objects.' [49] And again in 1837: 'So far from overestimating, I have no doubt, that the very services, which ought to recommend me to the country, and the qualities, which ought to give confidence, constitute insuperable objections to my election. Nothing can raise me short of saving the country from convulsions, which gives me not a moment of grief. I would rather, to use your own expression, stand alone in my glory, seeing what is coming, raising an honest and fearless voice of forewarning, untainted and untouched by the time, than to be President of these States, on any other condition than through a discharge of my duty.' [50]

IV

It is, then, clear enough that, in spite of any intrusions of mere human emotion, Calhoun must largely be regarded as a thinking apparatus, fitting the definition of Descartes as nearly as any one can.

There are three special phases which summarize this intellectual tendency most clearly and are worth reëmphasizing. First, there is the constant, subtle, elaborate speculation on finance and on the tariff. In this field Calhoun's ingenuity is undeniable, whatever may be thought of his conclusions. All that an outsider can say is, that the subject seems always to afford endless range to persons of the speculative temperament, and the theoretical handling of it is so surprisingly varied that one who is somewhat skeptical and very ill-informed is inclined to feel that the result of the speculation is, excellent arguments for everything and substantial reasons for nothing.

The question of slavery is different. Here we are dealing with broad human motives and passions more easily comprehensible. It is in the highest degree pathetic to see the zeal, the persistence, the unflagging confidence with which Calhoun fought the whole civilized world. He brings up every possible argument with astonishing vigor. Most of all he develops the old view, which was heard so often afterwards, that the millions of white slaves in the great industrial centers of England and the Northern States were far worse off than any black in the South. And as I read his cold, close-packed, dominating logic, my mind is all the time full of Aleck and 'the thirty lashes, well laid on.' I can feel every lash on my own back, till I wish Aleck could have laid them on the bare back of John C. Calhoun. Surely the man is an impressive tragic figure, thus opposing his unshaken courage and his magnificent reason to the inevitable, fatal movement of all modern thought.

The element of tragic struggle is evident also in the third of the great causes which Calhoun so heroically championed, and here there is a permanent and enduring significance that gives his effort and his figure a reality they might otherwise lack: I mean the cause of State Rights.

When the Federal Constitution was adopted, State sovereignty was a very real thing, and it appeared that a just and even balance between the two authorities, each working in its own sphere, was a happy and most valuable governmental invention. As Calhoun repeatedly and emphatically puts it: 'If there is one portion of the Constitution which I most admire, it is the distribution of power between the States and the general Government. . . . This is our invention and is altogether our own, and I consider it to be the greatest improvement which has been made in the science of government, after the division of power into the legislative, executive, and judicial.' [51] This relation of the Federal Government and the States appeared to him to constitute the best safeguard against tyranny of all sorts, and he believed that to maintain it in its original form was the first duty of a patriot.

But from the day the new government began to exist, the tendency to Federal encroachment was fatal. It might take different forms and be momentarily diverted, but its steady march was in the main unchecked. Calhoun saw the progress and foresaw the end, though even he could hardly have foreseen the immense impulse to centralization that would come from the Civil War and the utter crushing of the South. Various elements entered into this progress. The newer States, as they arose in the West, could not have the same traditional and historical State feeling. If you talk with a Westerner, he will have huge pride in his State as a locality, but little regard for it as a political entity. Common-sense has always worked in the same direction. Forty-eight different divorce laws, different systems of education, of jurisprudence, of regulation of the professions, will always seem to any practical man an intolerable nuisance, and he will welcome any effort at adjustment. And the notable thing is that every bit of power that is taken from the States and given to Washington deteriorates the State Governments and makes them less capable of exercising the power they have. The average citizen thinks of politics as centered at Washington and pays little attention to what happens in his State anyway. Worst of all, the ambition and ability of the country turn to Washington as their goal. It is remarkable that even Calhoun, like Webster, took little active part in State affairs. It was one of Patrick Henry's original objections to the Constitution that it would 'call forth the virtues and talents of America.' [52] And it may be suggested that the same objection would apply to the League of Nations, if it should ever become a dominant reality: genius and political ambition would be sucked away to Geneva and the vast concerns of national life would tend more and more to be left to corruption and incompetence.

One asks one's self, What is to come of it all? One is amazed that so few people seem to ask themselves seriously, What is to come of it all? For the unavoidable fact is that we have the State sovereignty, whether we like it or not. Most of our chief daily concerns are still regulated by the States. My father used to say, twenty years ago, that the average citizen could live a long life from birth to death without coming into contact with the Federal Government at all. Even twenty years have made extraordinary changes. Yet the State is still the practical sovereign for most of us. A good illustration of this is the lamentable affair of Sacco and Vanzetti. Here was an incident that aroused the world and might have involved the whole country in the most serious complications, perhaps even hostilities. Yet the Federal Government could not say a word or lift a finger to interfere with the justice of Massachusetts.

And again one asks, What is to come of it? Would it ever be possible to revive and reinvigorate the dignity and efficiency of the State Governments, as Calhoun preached and desired? If not, if the degeneration is inevitable, would it be better to make the whole thing over deliberately, and not continue the somewhat absurd process of facing backward and all the time rowing harder and more steadily forward? Yet the only possible way of

JOHN CALDWELL CALHOUN

fundamentally altering our system is through a
Constitutional Convention, and a Constitutional
Convention would be hell: every radical fanatic in
the world would be there, with a crazy scheme in
one pocket and a bomb in the other. And over
against this chaos stands the tall, gaunt figure of
John C. Calhoun, grandly and typically constant,
insisting with everlasting, imperturbable rational-
ity, that State Rights and State sovereignty are the
cure for everything.

To some of us politics, like religion and life itself,
are an eternal question. To Calhoun there were no
questions, or what there were had to be answered
at once and answered rightly.

IV
HORACE GREELEY

CHRONOLOGY

HORACE GREELEY

Born, Amherst, New Hampshire, February 3, 1811.
Became printer, 1826.
Went to New York, 1831.
Editor of *The New Yorker*, 1834–1840.
Married Mary Y. Cheney, July 5, 1836.
Established *The New York Tribune*, 1841, and edited it till his death.
In Congress, 1848.
Son Arthur died, 1849.
Nominated for the Presidency, 1872.
Wife died, 1872.
Died, New York, November 29, 1872.

HORACE GREELEY

HORACE GREELEY

I

THE nineteenth century developed many novel forces to affect the welfare of humanity. Of all these forces none was more significant or more far-reaching than popular journalism, and no name is more intimately connected with journalism than the name of Horace Greeley.

Greeley was all his life an intense and passionate worker. From his boyhood in the tens and twenties till his death in 1872, it was work, work, work, and nothing else. As a child in school and on the farm, he worked with his hands and with his brain. As a printer in New York, he worked with his brain and with his hands. As editor of *The New Yorker* and *The New York Tribune*, he worked with his brain, and still also with his busy fingers, till the fingers were weary and the brain worn to shreds.

Work was all of life that interested him, as was the case with so many Americans of his generation. What would you do unless you worked? You worked all the time, except when you were asleep. He had a physique which, on the whole, admirably seconded his intense activity. To be sure, his nerves were sensitive, played queer tricks with him, bothered him even from a child. He had fears and shrinkings and reluctances. Sharp and sudden noises terrified him. When the Fourth-of-July celebrations came, and guns were firing, the boy would run away and hide or thrust grass into his ears.[1] If he looked steadily through a closed window at falling rain, it induced nausea.[2] When there were stories of wolves about, he feared the dark and saw glowing eyeballs in every bush.[3] In later years the wolfish doings of men haunted the nerves also, and made sleep difficult, often impossible.

Yet, until he worked to unreasonable excess, his body served him well, and he did not suffer from that physical drag, which makes all work tormenting, if not impossible. Work was never tormenting to him, had become such a habit that he could hardly conceive the attraction of idleness. When he was in Paris, the gayety of the thoughtless, unoccupied crowd, soon palled upon him, disgusted him, and it appeared to him that a day of amusement was 'a routine that soon tells on one who is indurated in the habit of making the most of every working-hour.'[4] Even, with the peculiar egotism or personalism, which was so characteristic, he extended his own passion to humanity in general, and could not believe that all men did not love to work as he did: 'A lazy man, in my view, is always the pitiable victim of miseducation. Each human being, properly trained, works as freely and naturally as he eats; only the victims of parental neglect or misguidance hate work and prefer hunger and rags with idleness, to thrift won by industry and patient effort.' [5]

To men of Greeley's temperament work seems sufficient in itself, a reward and a delight, quite independent of any ulterior motive. They work from mere restless impulse, from the mechanical instinct of nerves and muscles to be used, almost regardless of any definite aim or object to be attained. At any rate, it may safely be said that at no time in his life was the earning of money in itself the incentive of Greeley's efforts. He earned and saved because that was the natural accompaniment of work, and because his foresight and far-sight felt the power of protection in such saving. But money meant little to him, because he lived sparely and hardly and had no taste for spending. His youth was the homely, rugged youth of the New England farmer's boy in the first half of the century. It was manly and independent, but it had all the elements of struggle and privation and precious little of comfort or cosseting. His father worked desperately hard, but luck went against him. He was burdened with debt, always in financial trouble, and could give his children little but the bare necessaries. The bare necessaries were all that Horace was accustomed to and apparently all he ever wanted. In the poverty of those early years were established the oddities of dress which became so peculiarly associated with him that men rarely think of him without them. As a boy, even when he began to earn, he would spend nothing on clothes. He went into New York with the crudest country garments, and he had no disposition to shed them even under the pressure of ridicule. All his life he dressed roughly, uncouthly, ineptly, wore trailing coats and trailing trousers and clumsy boots, and his slouch hat and white overcoat were objects of everlasting caricature. He was clean, and insisted that he was, and sometimes he repelled the attacks of the satirists with a certain petulance: 'All this time the object of this silly raillery has doubtless worn better clothes than two thirds of those who thus assailed him — better than any of them could honestly wear, if they paid their debts otherwise than by bankruptcy; while, if they are indeed more cleanly than he, they must bathe very thoroughly

not less than twice a day.' ⁶ But it is likely that, in
later years at any rate, he rather cultivated eccentricity in dress, feeling obscurely that it enhanced
his democratic hold upon the affections of the
public, and not feeling that there must be something artificial in a hold that required to be enhanced in such a fashion.

Even with a family and a city household of his
own, it appears that Greeley maintained the same
Spartan régime that had taken possession of his
spirit for good and all. No doubt the wife and children had the necessaries and many of the comforts.
But they were trained to consider luxury as super-
fluous, if not wicked, and to believe that only the
idle needed to spend money in order to be happy.
Yet he was fond of his children, devoted to them,
and spoke of them with singular tenderness. The
boy Arthur, familiarly known as 'Pickie,' who was
such a favorite of Margaret Fuller's, is described
at length in Greeley's autobiography, with a pathetic, lingering fondness, and his death was for
the time a prostrating blow. When a visitor called
on the great editor, the busy man, who was late for
his appointment anyway, excused himself, as he
rushed into the house, '"Just let me run up and
see my babies *one* minute; I haven't seen 'em all

day, you know"; and he sprang up the stairs two
steps at a time. I heard him talk in high glee to the
children in the room for just "one minute" and
then he rejoined me.'⁷

More and more, as I study the lives of men of
prominence, or of any men, for that matter, do I
feel the curiosity of studying their wives, and it is
evident that Greeley's wife played a considerable
part in his career, though we can get at her only
very indirectly and obscurely. Here and there
comes a touch that makes her stand out. For instance, we are told that, when Greeley married her,
she was a teacher and was 'crazy for knowledge.'
How clearly you see the type! And you can understand that she could put up with her husband's
oddities, perhaps had plenty of her own. He declares that she strictly carried out his wishes as
to plain living.⁸ She sympathized with the dietary
fancies which he acquired from the once celebrated
Graham and drove away guests by putting them in
practice.⁹ When he bought a farm, she insisted
upon three requisites, a spring, a brook, and
woods.¹⁰ Her rigid family discipline is drolly illustrated in the account of Governor Seward's attempt to smoke on the premises. 'Now Mrs.
Greeley happened to be ill in a room just above

that in which the gentlemen were, and her husband
knew that just so soon as the cigar-smoke should
make its way to her nostrils, through the flue of the
chimney, she would descend upon them like an
avalanche in whatever costume she happened just
then to be.' Wherefore Seward with his cigar was
coaxed out into the street and kept promenading
for an hour in astonished perplexity as to the
cause of such inhospitable treatment.[11] Another
vivid scene occurred when Greeley was arrested in
Paris at the suit of an injured sculptor who had
sent a statue to the New York Exposition. Mrs.
Greeley insisted upon following her husband to jail
to get a full explanation of the matter.[12] But, whatever her oddities, she was a loyal and a helpful
wife, and the loss of her, just as Greeley had failed
in his last great political struggle, was too much to
bear. 'In the darkest hour my suffering wife left
me, none too soon, for she had suffered too deeply
and too long. I laid her in the ground with hard
dry eyes.' [13] The memory that lingers with me
most is that she was 'crazy for knowledge.' What
a profound and pitiable epitaph!

Work and the domestic affections — these seem
to have been all of Greeley's life. It is remarkable
to see how the other common interests of mankind

are left out or slighted. All the references to his boyhood agree in indicating that he had no taste for play, never cared to join in childish sports or amusements. He was fond of fishing, but, as his biographer remarks, he fished not for fun, but for fish.[14] He liked to roam the woods: why? Because he found wild honey, and wild honey was marketable.[15] He did like to play checkers, and played it well, and so hard that it ceased to be play and became work, like everything else. Also, he played cards occasionally, though never for money and never on Sunday. Anyway, such things were a waste of time and rather to be frowned upon, and 'he advised persons of sedentary habits to shun them "because of the inevitable tendency to impair digestion and incite headache."' [16] Certainly the people of that generation took life seriously.

It was the same with all the more elaborate distractions which are supposed to divert maturer age. Travel? Oh, yes, the man traveled, but it is clear that he was always in a hurry, and always accumulating copy for *The Tribune*. Social life? If you got him with people whom he liked and let him have all the conversation, he would talk and talk well. But he had no taste for ordinary social gatherings, and avoided them, and did not appear to advantage

in them. His dress was inappropriate, his manners
were brusque. When he was growing up, he stuck
to his boarding-house, never went out of an evening
and had no one come to see him. The habit per-
sisted in later years. How could you work and waste
time on mere frivolity? As for the adjuncts of
cheerful social life, smoking and drinking, he held
them in horror. Alcohol he never touched, and discouraged others from touching it. And you can't
say much more of the evil of tobacco than this:
'The chewing, smoking, or snuffing of tobacco has
seemed to me, if not the most pernicious, certainly
the vilest, most detestable abuse of his corrupted
sensual appetites whereof depraved Man is capable.' [17] Whew!

What are usually considered more refined pleasures had little better luck with such an instinctive
Puritan. He tolerated the fine arts and patronized
them and filled his house with pictures; [18] but I
doubt if he ever looked at them. He admitted the
charm of the theater and its capabilities, [19] but deplored its vices and attacked it furiously in his
paper. [20] 'The wise man,' he says, 'is he who goes
but once to the theater, and keeps the impression
then made on his mind fresh and clear to the close
of life.' [21] Come to think of it, the idea is a rather

good one, and when I remember my first visit to the theater I almost wish I had acted upon Greeley's precept. Even Nature, from the æsthetic point of view, meant little more to this ardent farmer than it does to most farmers: crops and bugs and manure loomed larger than sunsets, and his agricultural writings are distinctly and overwhelmingly practical.

When you look into it, you find the same is true of books. Greeley was an enormous reader from childhood. He was always at a book or a newspaper, read in the woods, or on his way from school, or by the fireside at night. He began to read abnormally young, with the book suspended on his mother's knee so that he incidentally acquired the rather singular aptitude of reading with the book upside down.[22] But, while in youth he read anything that came handy, literature proper or anything else, his taste was wholly practical, and the practical was all he got from all he read. Homer was dull to him,[23] as to a good many others, and Shakespeare was a Tory and an aristocrat.[24] He wanted education to be practical, and preached that it should be so, wanted it to turn out farmers and artisans who should understand their business and like it. Colleges, which he had never frequented, seemed to

him to be dangerous, at least greatly in need of
reform. 'We must have seminaries which not
merely provide work [manual work] for their
pupils, but *require* it inflexibly from all.' [25] Work,
work, always work! And no doubt work is an admirable thing; but when you pack life too full and
solid with it, something is apt to explode somewhere.

II

Yet the work in Greeley's case was certainly not
for himself alone, nor, though eminently practical,
was it by any means always material in its aims or
nature. His mind was constantly busy, and often
in abstract thinking, though always with a practical bearing and purpose. His intelligence was
almost preternaturally quick and active, a swift
sequence of skipping, frisking, cavorting thoughts,
which kept both the inner and outer cosmos in a
perpetual stir and whirl. He himself speaks of his
'invincible willingness to be made wiser to-day than
I was yesterday,' [26] which is a very pretty way of
putting it, and the willingness readily extended to
imparting the wisdom to others. At the same time,
the thinking was not always very logical or very
deep. It was that of the self-made, self-taught man,

who acquires readily and widely, but without much system or much exact training in the use of thought. Also, Greeley not only did not gain mental control; he lacked it naturally, was erratic, easily led and misled, and duped by himself more often and more disastrously than by others. It is most instructive to compare him with Franklin, whom he resembles in his printing aptitudes as well as in many other respects. Both had marked intellectual limitations, both had a singular shrewd common-sense. But Franklin's common-sense rarely, if ever failed him, while Greeley's was perpetually subject to unfortunate and almost unaccountable lapses.

In the more lofty regions of thought Greeley counted for little or nothing. Religion did not trouble him much, or, in its higher emotional aspects, greatly concern him. When he was a child, the darker phases of Calvinism repelled and distressed him. The old puzzle of an omnipotent God who made his creatures to suffer eternally would not let him rest. And he finally solved it by the comfortable doctrines of Universalism. If men did evil, they must be punished, certainly. But it was unreasonable to suppose that the punishment would last forever, and, if it was unreasonable, it was untrue.[27] In any case, his genial and serene spirit was not going to vex itself with problems beyond its competence or that of any one. For a time he was curious about Spiritualism; but this too evaporated. The long and the short of it was that, as he said in later years, 'I am so taken up with the things of this world, that I have too little time to spend on the affairs of the other.' [28] He was a faithful church-goer, but seemed to think that his bodily presence was the main essential, and allowed his mind to profit by such golden opportunities for sleep. 'He generally stalked in rather early, the pockets of his long white coat filled with newspapers, and, immediately on taking his seat, went to sleep. As soon as service began, he awoke, looked first to see how many vacant places were in the pew, and then, without a word, put out his long arm into the aisle and with one or two vigorous scoops, pulled in a sufficient number of strangers standing there to fill all the vacancies; then he slept again.' [29]

There you have the man: whatever benefits the church or anything else gave him must be shared with others, and the sharing was rather more important than the benefits. The side of religion that appealed to him was the practical, and the most fruitful field of labor for his vastly laborious spirit was work for others. The inconsistencies of professedly religious people on this point were extremely repugnant to him and he could not satisfy himself of 'the rightfulness and consistency of a Christian's spending $5000 to $10,000 a year on the appetites and enjoyments of himself and his family, when there are a thousand families within a mile of him who are compelled to live on less than $200 a year.' [30] His own personal benevolence was almost unlimited. He gave and especially he lent widely, freely, many persons thought, foolishly. Yet if he was often duped, he was not fooled; that is, he fell into the trap with his eyes open, and knew that he was complying with Christian charity rather than with deserving need. The vagrant hundreds who wanted to borrow always promised to pay. 'Sometimes I have lent the sum required; in other cases, I have refused it; but I cannot remember *a single instance* in which the promise to repay was made good.' [31] And when a cause did not interest him or appeal to him, he could refuse with a decided petulance, and even with the curious coarse vigor of language which his wandering youth had engrafted upon his age, as when he replied to the man who appealed for a subscription to 'a cause which will prevent a thousand of our fellow-beings from going to hell,' 'I will not give you a cent. There don't half enough go there now.' [32]

Greeley not only gave money, but advice, and in incredible measure. As a popular editor, the demands upon him in this regard were enormous, but he gladly spent his time and strength in meeting them. Margaret Fuller, who lived in his family and knew him intimately and, after her fashion, critically, said of him, 'With the exception of my own mother, I think him the most disinterestedly generous person I have ever known.' [33] The advice was often roughly and broadly given, as in the celebrated 'Go West, young man, go West!' or as in the more concrete story of the boy who had been living with his sister, had quarreled with her and left her and came into the office to ask for assistance. Greeley kept on writing and did not even look up. 'Is your sister married?' 'Yes.' 'Is she respectable?' 'Certainly, sir.' 'Go straight to your sister and tell her that you are ashamed of yourself, and ask her forgiveness. If she will take you, go back and live with her; and after this remember that if your own sister is not your friend, you will not be likely to find any friend in New York City.' [34] The boy went, and Greeley went on writing. He was too busy for gentleness; but his advice, though as in this case sometimes hit or miss, was generally sound and wholesome, and those who took it profited.

He was just as ready to advise the world at large as any individual, and his editorial employment gave him a magnificent opportunity for doing so. He had the essential qualities of the born reformer, the immense energy, the quick and ready, if superficial sympathy, the unfailing enthusiasm, the limitless confidence in himself. To be sure, he insists that there was an element of the conservative in him, and no doubt there was, as in all of us, 'conservative by instinct, by tradition.' [35] He liked the practical way of doing things, or what he considered such. But above all he had the passion for making over the dull old world and never could let it alone.

Various reforms appealed to him; in fact, nearly all reforms, so long as they were practical and could be felt and touched. On one point, indeed, he resented modern progress, if it be progress, on the point of divorce. He was at all times a strenuous supporter of what he considered ideal family life. But he wanted prohibition, he wanted education reorganized, he worked with tireless zeal for the abolition of slavery. Above all, he was constantly and consistently interested in improving the conditions of labor and the general status of the poor. It is curious to see all the nostrums and panaceas of our own day — and a thousand years ago — trumpeted in the middle of the last century, with the same eternal confidence and undying hope. It is true that Greeley was in some respects moderate. He never urged the fundamental disturbance of the right of property. But he was fascinated by schemes of association, long and ardently advocated Fourierism, and believed that if men of all types and classes would only meet each other and work together in good faith, the worst of human evils might be overcome. And from the practical side it may at least be said that he anticipated much of the coöperative tendency in which social reform has made the most decided gains.

It must be admitted that in philanthropy, as in other things, he was easily duped. 'The "long-haired men and short-haired women" of the country seemed at times to have him entirely under their sway,' says Andrew D. White.[36] They took his money, they took his time, they took his influence. Yet it is impossible not to admire the noble fervor of his longing to do practical, concrete good, 'to lift the Laboring Class as such — not out of labor, by any means — but out of ignorance, inefficiency, dependence, and want, and place them in a position of partnership and recognized mutual helpfulness with the suppliers of the Capital which they render fruitful and efficient.' [37]

And as he had the zeal of the born reformer, so he had the superb, unfailing optimism. You can see it written in his face. The author of the 'Essays of Elia' proposed to hire a stone-cutter to set up a monument, on which should be engraved, 'Here Charles Lamb loved his fellow-men.' Greeley needed no stone-cutter: he carried his monument with him, in those benignant features from which even thirty years of New York journalism could not erase the delightful rustic candor, in that fringe of sparse white whisker, which always leaves one doubting between an inverted halo and a tonsorial negligence. And he expressed his immense belief in the future and in humanity not only with his countenance but with his pen: 'I see no reason why the wildest dreams of the fanatical believer in Human Progress and Perfectibility may not ultimately be realized, and each child so trained as to shun every vice, aspire to every virtue, attain the highest practicable skill in Art and efficiency in Industry, loving and pursuing honest, untasked labor for the health, vigor, and peace of mind thence resulting, as well as for its more palpable rewards, and joyfully recognizing in universal the only assurance of individual good.' [38] When a man carries such sentiments in his heart, he may surely be excused for wearing optimistic whiskers.

III

It was unavoidable that Greeley's philanthropy should draw him into practical politics, though it would have been far better for his reputation if this had not happened. On abstract political questions he always had a definite opinion and an energetic one. He early devoted himself to the extreme protectionist theory and worked for it to the end. His opposition to slavery in the fifties probably made him more friends than anything else, as well as more enemies, and in that earlier period he was a useful and effective agent. But when the Civil War broke out, it was too much for him. He was distracted between humanity, love of the Union, hatred of slavery, hatred of war, and his general disposition to dictate to everybody on everything. First he was for letting the South go; then for prosecuting the war and emancipating the slaves; then, when the struggle dragged on, he was for making peace, by foreign mediation if necessary; then after it was all over for forgiving every-body, especially Jefferson Davis, whose bail-bond he eagerly signed. Sometimes he pleaded with Lincoln, sometimes he bullied him, sometimes he rejected him as a poor creature. And always *The Tribune* was an enormous power in the country, which whirled millions after its vagaries, and forced the President to consider its editor, even when he could not agree with him, as when he allowed Greeley to carry on peace negotiations in Canada. It is impossible not to contrast Greeley's flighty inconsistencies with Lincoln's deliberate and statesman-like opportunism. Yet under all the inconsistencies lay the fundamental patriotic feeling and high-mindedness which Lincoln appraised when he wrote to Wilson, 'I do not know how you estimate Greeley, but I consider him incapable of corruption or falsehood.' [39]

But when it came to personal participation in political activity, Greeley was even less successful than in theorizing. It is clear that he was in no way adapted to direct political success. He was a good speaker — that is, he always had something to say, and said it in vigorous and intelligible language; but even on the platform his oddities must have interfered with the magnetic control of an audience. And in dealing with individuals the oddities and defects were far more pronounced. He had no magnetism at all, and it often seemed as if he had no manners. He irritated people and fretted them and rubbed them the wrong way. In those rough days this would often have resulted in personal conflict, if Greeley had been anything of a fighter. He was not. He had his courage, but it was of the passive order. When he was a boy, he would not stand up and fight. 'When attacked, he would neither fight nor run away, "but stand still and take it."' [40] And this is exactly what he did when he was assaulted in Washington by a political enemy. He used his tongue savagely, without knowing it; he did not know how to use his fists, and did not care to.

Yet, with all these disqualifications, he was always eager for public office, always felt that he could be useful to his fellows in that way and wanted the chance. At any rate, he wanted to be asked. As he himself naïvely put it: 'I should like the idea of running for an office without the necessity of getting beaten on the one hand or being swallowed up in official cares and duties on the other.' [41] Many of us would like political distinction on those somewhat impossible terms.

Greeley's political desires and interests were
much fostered by his association with Weed and
Seward, the greatest political forces in the New
York of that day. Weed early appreciated the
value of Greeley's journalistic ability and made the
most of it, but it soon became apparent that the
qualities of a great editor were not necessarily those
of a great administrator and neither Weed nor his
chief manifested any eagerness for getting their
friend into office. Greeley resented this and finally
broke off all relations in the well-known letter dis-
solving the partnership of Weed, Seward, and
Greeley. A little later his vehement opposition did
as much as anything to prevent Seward from being
nominated for the presidency in 1860. The episode
as a whole is not an attractive phase of Greeley's
career.

The only case of Greeley's actually taking part
in governmental work was his filling an unexpired
term in the House of Representatives in 1848. His
brief activity in this instance was bustling at any
rate, if not glorious. He at once started an active
investigation of the mileage allowances for members of Congress, which was no doubt well inten-
tioned and beneficial, but did not increase his personal popularity. In his Congressional career, as

in everything, you see his vigorous self-assertion, his genuine desire to do good to everybody, and his complete disregard of what happened to anybody's feelings in the process.

In 1872, Greeley secured a presidential nomination. Grant was the regular Republican candidate, but there had been much disapproval of his first term, and the discontented Republicans got together at Cincinnati and nominated Greeley, who was also later nominated by the Democrats. There was something so ludicrously inconsistent about this procedure that it made the campaign almost a farce, though a bitter one. Greeley had spent his life abusing the Southern slaveholders and the absurdity and hollowness of their supporting him could hardly be veiled by any pretext of 'shaking hands across the bloody chasm.' The difficulty of the position and his eagerness for success led Greeley into alliance with a set of inferior politicians who took advantage of his easy good-nature and gave anything but favorable promise of what his administration was likely to be, if he were elected. The contest was cruelly personal in many respects, and the savage efforts of the cartoonists, notably of Thomas Nast, in opposition to Greeley, gave it a vivid grossness which has rarely been surpassed. Greeley was not only beaten, but over-whelmed. As he himself expressed it, 'I was the worst beaten man that ever ran for high office. And I have been assailed so bitterly that I hardly know whether I was running for the Presidency or the Penitentiary.' [42] The strain, the fatigue, and the bitterness of the struggle were too much for nerves already overworked and further shaken by the loss of his wife, and within a month after his defeat Greeley was dead.

The element of ambition in Greeley's character has been a good deal discussed and disputed. But it is evident that, like most of us, he wanted to suc-ceed in whatever he undertook. He disclaimed the ambition for authorship. Yet he probably liked to think that the 'Recollections of a Busy Life' and especially 'The American Conflict' were consider-able books. They are in size, but hardly in other respects. In the same way he disclaimed political ambition. Yet he felt that he had good ideas, great ideas, on governmental matters, the immense flat-tery that always waits upon popular editorship had to some extent turned his head, and he believed that he would make as good a president as another man, perhaps much better. In 1868 he wrote of Webster, 'Great, intellectually, as Daniel Webster was, he would have been morally greater, and every way more useful and honored, had he sternly responded, "Get thee behind me, Satan!" to every suggestion that he might yet attain the Presidency.' [43] Exactly the same thing might have been written of Greeley in 1872. What would have happened if he had been elected it is difficult to guess. As in other cases, high responsibility might have toned him down and made him practical and useful. But one has one's doubts. It is a familiar boast with our mothers that any American can get the presidency, and sometimes, when one scans the long list of incumbents, one is tempted to think that any American has got it. Certainly many types have occupied the sacred chair, from genius to gentlemanly insignificance; but there are not many, outside the State's prison, which is rather unfairly excluded, more incompatible with it than the fiery, versatile, garrulous, emotional, whimsical editor of a New York paper.

IV

All the same, he was a great editor. The cheap, popular newspaper came into prominence and power just about as Greeley reached manhood, and he took to it naturally and completely. From a child he wanted to be a printer, and he had a passion for reading the papers. As soon as he could get his elbows free from the fiercest necessity of self-support, he became an editor, first of *The New Yorker*, then of the political and partisan *Log Cabin*, then of *The Tribune*, which was the child of his efforts and the mother of his fame.

He grew as the paper grew, grew as journalism grew, grew as New York grew, developed daily and yearly in self-possession and self-assertion, if not in self-comprehension. On the merely business side of his undertaking he was not especially distinguished. I do not find his name associated with any of the marvelous mechanical discoveries which so greatly facilitated the dissemination of newspapers as the years went on, nor do I note that he was especially interested in these. Neither was he a great or successful financier. His magnificent thrift and self-control, his steady and well-directed industry, enabled him to hold his own, even when unsupported. But the difficulties were enormous and almost overwhelmed him. He worked all day and nearly all night, drove everything and everybody about him. Yet, even so, it was a struggle to keep the credit going and the bills paid. 'I paid off everybody tonight, had $10 dollars left, and have $350 to raise on

Monday. Borrowing places all sucked dry. I shall
raise it, however.' ⁴⁴ This, on a larger and larger
scale, was the story, until McElrath came along
and undertook the business management of the
affair. It was the salvation of Greeley, and after
that he had nothing to think of but his pen. *The
Tribune* grew to be a vast investment, and its editor
was always provided for on the financial side. True
to his theories, he insisted on introducing the co-
operative element, and the paper was early made
into a stock company, with opportunity for all who
worked for it to share in the ownership. Moreover,
Greeley was eager to secure, and did secure able
assistants in various lines; yet I do not gather that
he was especially popular or beloved by his subordinates, and his quick and arbitrary habits drove
off the ablest of them, Raymond and Dana.

Nor does it appear that Greeley was particularly
active in the advertising department, though he
well understood the importance of it, even in the
primitive days, before Barnum and others had
developed the full resources of publicity. What
impressed Greeley chiefly at the beginning was the
danger of the advertising element. Once allow yourself to be subsidized by rich and unscrupulous advertisers, and what becomes of the independence of

journalism? In its extreme form he censures this
tendency bitterly, speaking of the 'very large and
popularly respectable class of journals, which regularly hire out their columns, editorial and advertising, for the enticement of their readers to visit
groggeries, theaters, horse-races, as we sometimes
have thoughtlessly done, but hope never, unless
through deplored inadvertence, to do again.' [45] And
at a later date Godkin highly praises *The Tribune's*
independent attitude: 'He sacrificed everything,
advertisers, subscribers, and all else, to what he
considered principle.' [46] At a later date still there
came a change. The growth of business, the subtle
and insinuating pressure of politics, forced Greeley
to abandon his lofty position to some extent, never
certainly in theory or in his own view, but distinctly in the unprejudiced opinion of others. His
support of Barnard's New York ring was considered
by Godkin to be of interested character, and the
editor of *The Nation* even goes so far in a private
letter as to assert that 'Greeley is as time-serving
and ambitious and scheming an old fellow as any of
them.' [47] His tolerance of the Tweed régime was
as servile as that of the other papers, until *The
Times* shook them into unavoidable action.[48] Here
again, however, it is obvious that Greeley was

duped, partly by clever machinations, partly by his own ambition and enthusiasm.

The news side of the paper was more in Greeley's province than the advertising. In this regard it is interesting to note his desire for and insistence upon accuracy. He was scrupulous as to form, emphasizing the importance of clear and readable English. He was scrupulous as to fact, at all times endeavoring to get a clear account of what really happened and then to stick to it. He condemned sensational journalism, even going so far as to say that the 'violent hurt inflicted upon social order and individual happiness' by the lurid account of a murder involved greater guilt than that of the murderer himself,[49] which is going pretty far, though perhaps not too far. The efforts of journalistic enterprise displayed by *The Tribune* in its competition for news with the other New York papers make amusing reading, when compared with the greater facilities of to-day, and sometimes extreme eagerness resulted in some absurd hoax, like that of the mythical Battle of Slievenamon in Ireland, which was duly reported in *The Tribune* and ridiculed elsewhere as the Battle of Slievegammon. All the same, Greeley was a live editor, in news-vending as in other respects.

But it was in the editorial columns that his main strength lay, and from the start he had an intense appreciation of the power that was just beginning to develop in the popular press and the future that lay before it. This power was completely a growth of the nineteenth century and it is doubtful whether any one has yet analyzed its full nature or extent. To some persons its benefits and advantages must appear more questionable than they did to Greeley, and there are certainly evils which Greeley was disposed to underrate or overlook. For instance, the newspaper has been anti-religious, not so much in direct attack, which is not usual in America, as in a subtle undermining of the influence of the church and the pulpit. A hundred and fifty years ago, if you wanted to hear what was going on in the world, you went to church and the minister told you everything you ought to know, and you believed him. Now you stay at home and read the newspaper: you may not believe, but you are influenced. Again, the newspaper is anti-social. Before it came, men got the news by word of mouth and had to find and meet each other to get it. Now you learn more by staying at home in quiet and silence. But little drawbacks like these were nothing in the enthusiasm which Greeley felt for the newspaper as a universal, democratic, educative force. When he was invited to go before an English Parliamentary committee and discuss the subject of journalism, he told the committee that he considered the newspaper 'worth all the schools in the country. I think it creates a taste for reading in every child's mind, and it increases his interest in his lessons.' [50]

Which is certainly another proof of the man's indomitable optimism. But he at any rate did his best to make the editorial influence what he would have had it, to use it to develop and educate and bring out what was best and noblest in the great American people, whom he labored in his way to serve with all his heart and all his energy. Listen to his summing-up of editorial requisites: 'An ear ever open to the plaints of the wronged and the suffering, though they can never repay advocacy, and those who mainly support newspapers will be annoyed and often exposed by it; a heart as sensitive to oppression and degradation in the next street as if they were practiced in Brazil or Japan; a pen as ready to expose and reprove the crimes whereby wealth is amassed and luxury enjoyed in our own country at this hour, as if they had only been committed by Turks or Pagans in Asia some centuries ago.' [51] This is a high ideal for a journalist, and if

Greeley did not always live up to it, he could hardly be expected to. He carried it in his heart at any rate, which was something.

To be sure, his methods seem to us singularly at variance with his standards. He had heard too much of a rough and brutal style of speech in his youth, and he never got over it. Coarse and ugly terms applied to adversaries with careless inconsideration never really help, and Greeley was too prone to them. He used profanity in his private talk and the equivalent of profanity in his editorials. These things made hard feeling, sometimes even resulted in legal proceedings, as in the case of the celebrated Cooper libel suits. They were a disfiguring element which cannot be overlooked.

At the same time, they came partly from his qualities of power. Words were natural to him, and he poured them out almost unthinkingly, ugly as well as graceful, bitter as well as sweet. His style has been extravagantly praised by excellent judges, notably by Godkin.[52] It seems to me diffuse and by no means of the highest literary quality; but it is ,certainly vivid and energetic. He had no humor, because he never had the humorous, detached view of life: everything was too intensely and immediately absorbing to him. But he had a quick, apt wit in giving things a mocking or a satirical turn, after the somewhat exaggerated fashion of Mark Twain. His intellectual powers, while, as we have before seen, not profoundly penetrating, were quick and agile, and ready to turn at any moment to any subject. Above all, he was inexhaustible in fertility of argument, had that splendid confidence in human reason, especially his own, which some of us are born without, but which seems to be almost indispensable to the successful editor. He liked to argue, actually enjoyed it, would argue about anything. He liked opposition, liked to have people differ from him: it gave him a chance to show and especially to feel his own power. And he was reluctant to give up an opinion; he hated above all things to own that he was in the wrong.

With these editorial qualities he endeared himself to the vast masses of the American people and became perhaps the most notable of all the great personal editors of the middle of the nineteenth century. That personal element in the handling of a paper seems now, for various reasons, largely to have passed away. Curiously enough, the personal was intimately bound up with the impersonal. Beyond question what gave the editorial columns their singular power was chiefly their anonymity.

You might laugh at Jones's opinions, or Smith's; but the editor's — that was different. The large type and the lack of signature somehow seemed to compel respect. So, though men knew it was Horace Greeley, he of the white coat and old hat, who was writing, his editorial words seemed to get a larger significance. And the impersonality at once developed egotism and was benefited by it. You could not help feeling yourself to be a big man when you were swaying the minds of millions, and the bigger you felt yourself, the more you swayed.

Some such feeling of almost godlike consequence certainly inspired the soul of Horace Greeley, and he carried round with him in later years the sense of personifying one of the greatest forces and achievements of his century. This is clearly seen in the striking passage in which he describes his relation to his journal: 'Fame is a vapor; popularity an accident; riches take wings; the only earthly certainty is oblivion; no man can foresee what a day may bring forth; while those who cheer to-day will often curse to-morrow; and yet I cherish the hope that the journal I have projected and established will live and flourish long after I shall have mouldered into forgotten dust; . . . and that the stone which covers my ashes may bear to future eyes the still intelligible inscription, "Founder of *The New York Tribune*." [53]

It must be admitted, as Greeley himself admitted, that the glory belonging to his journalistic enterprise is of a somewhat ephemeral and temporary character; it is like that of the actor, or the athlete, immense for the moment and immediately savored, but transitory and quickly forgotten as a dream. Yet when one looks about one at the enormous flood of literary production, and realizes how slight is the chance of any slow or careful work, or any hidden genius, ever making its way to permanence through such a throng of competitors, one wonders whether, perhaps, after all, immediate renown, like Greeley's, is not better than the effort to create a masterpiece which posterity may or may not worship. Only some of us would rather cherish the dream of the masterpiece.

At any rate, Greeley made *The Tribune*, and swayed America, and passed away. In his solemn and impressive funeral all antagonisms were forgotten. The New York papers, which a month before had been ready to put him in jail, united in eulogy, the President, the Vice-President, and the Vice-President elect rode in one carriage behind the hearse. And it was only fair that these honors should be showered upon his ending; for the poor man was dead before the breath was out of his body, dead, utterly dead. Shakespeare tells us that

'The evil that men do lives after them,
The good is oft interred with their bones.'

Greeley had done no evil, or none to speak of, and the good he did, extensive and indisputable as it was, was not of a character to make the world revere his memory.

V
EDWIN BOOTH

CHRONOLOGY

EDWIN THOMAS BOOTH

    Born, Belair, Maryland, November 13, 1833.

    First appearance, Boston Museum, 1849.

    Went to California, 1852.

    Married Mary Devlin, July 7, 1860.

    Wife died, February, 1863.

    Booth's Theater opened, February 3, 1869.

    Married Mary F. McVicker, June 7, 1869.

    Went into bankruptcy, 1874.

    Wife died, November 13, 1881.

    Last appearance, April, 1891.

    Died, Players Club, New York, June 8, 1893.

EDWIN BOOTH

EDWIN BOOTH

I

THE most real of all human figures are the creations of the imagination. The nearest approach
to earthly immortality, to an existence that is not
shattered or imperiled by failure or decay, belongs
to spirits that have never lived in the flesh, but
have been embodied by great artists in dream
shapes that have taken an enduring hold upon the
fancy and the memory of humanity. Helen, Hector,
and Achilles, Dido and Æneas, Hamlet, Lear,
Rosalind and Portia, live and will live, when millions who have known and loved them have been
buried and forgotten. To have attached your name
to such a figure, as creator, or even as impersonator,
is to attach something of its permanence to the
fragile nonentity of a trivial creature of clay.

Naturally the actor's name does not live like the
author's. Yet a great actor is long identified with
the parts he most loved to represent, and few actors
have been so completely identified with their stage
counterparts as Edwin Booth with Hamlet. Those
who remember Booth will always think of him as
the Prince of Denmark and the two names will long

be linked together in the history of the American stage. Indeed Booth's life was essentially that of the actor and the artist. Born on a lonely Maryland farm in 1833, he was educated partly by solitude and partly by the erratic genius of his father, who was in some respects a greater actor than he. He began early to act himself, led for some years the vagrant, bohemian life which seems appropriate to the profession, married first one actress, then another, interpreted Shakespeare to America and Germany, and appeared for the last time as Hamlet in 1891, two years before his death.

But, though an actor, Booth was eminently and thoroughly a man and not a stage puppet. He was full of human sensibility, passion, and thought, and was as interesting and lovable in private life as upon the stage. He did not, indeed, have much concern with the current movement of the world outside of his art. His most active connection with politics was through his younger brother's mad assassination of Lincoln, which for a time threatened to destroy Edwin's future altogether. But, though no politician, he himself was a loyal American, a lover of the Union, and above all a democrat in theory and practice.

To be sure, he did not mix easily with his fellow-

men at large. He had no gift of light, gay cordiality
with strangers; on the contrary, when he came into
the company of such, he shrank into himself and
would neither make advances nor receive them.
This is emphasized by those who knew him best.
'He had stage-fright everywhere but on the stage,'
says Mr. Royle. '. . . He was abnormally shy, de-
tested social gatherings, positively suffered under
scrutiny, and the few who casually met him got the
impression that he was uncommonly inept. This
impression he never took the slightest pains to correct.' [1] 'In the world he had a way of shrinking
into himself that gave him a reputation for shyness
and reserve,' says Sullivan.[2] And Winter speaks of
'Edwin Booth, who became like a marble statue
upon the advent of a stranger.' [3]

Booth's own testimony as to this shyness and
social shrinking is even more interesting. How
vivid in its careless revelation is his account of a
meeting with a former acquaintance: 'He spoke to
me the first day out; has his wife with him — pleasant sort of body. Says he has lived all these years
in England. Asked after you, and there our conversation dropped — my fault, I suppose.' [4]

Whoever the fault, the social failure was there,
haunting, insistent, wearisome. Booth himself at-

tributed it partly to his bringing-up. His father liked solitude and sought it. 'Hence, his wife and children became isolated, and were ill at ease in the presence of other than their own immediate relatives.' ⁵ General society was always a bore, often a source of distinct distress. 'I remember him,' says Ellsworth, 'standing with folded arms in a corner, talking little. He told me that such a party was agony to him, for his hearing was so painfully acute that he could hear even a whisper across the room.' ⁶ And he said to Mr. Royle, 'I love those best who let me alone.' ⁷

Yet this dislike of the world at large did not preclude the most delicate sympathy and understanding. The small change of social conversation is apt to consist of censorious gossip, and Booth made it a rule to avoid criticism of others that, when conveyed to their ears, might wound and alienate. Moreover, he had a profound sense of suffering and sorrow, and he was unsparing in his efforts to relieve them. Money he was lavish of. 'To my certain knowledge he gave away in charity more than most men would consider a fortune,' says Mr. Bispham.⁸ But the giving was so quiet and unostentatious that few were aware of it. 'I have seen him blush like a girl at the receipt of a letter of

thanks, and run away like a coward from the grati-
tude of those he had helped.' ⁹ And the kindness
went further than money. He put himself in others'
places, appreciated their needs and cravings, and
supplied them. An actor whom he had long known
revolted at the thought of retirement into an institution, so Booth 'made a place for the old fellow
at his own theater as long as he lived.' ¹⁰ He went
further still and taught his daughter that humility
and gentleness are the true principle of elevation:
'Self-respect, politeness, and gentleness in all things
and to all persons will give you sufficient dignity.' ¹¹

This tender consideration, which is so charming
in Booth, showed in his treatment of animals as
well as of men and women. I find no mention of
his fishing or hunting, but that is perhaps part of
the curious absence of all active sport from even
his boyhood. Horses he loved, loved to drive them
and to drive good ones, and he seems to have understood them thoroughly. For other animals, both
wild and domestic, he had a peculiar sympathy and
especially a desire to avoid giving them pain. In
his youth his father brought him up to abstain from
animal food and, though this did not persist, the
habit of tenderness did. Mr. Winter has a curious
story of his having poisoned some flies and having

been at first amused at the singular effect on them. '"But suddenly I realized that, as death was not instantaneous, they must be suffering, and I have been grieved about it ever since." There was no affectation in this. His remorse was genuine and it was painful to see.' [12]

Though Booth had so great an aversion to strangers, he had many intimate friends, many who knew him long and well, and loved him better the more they knew him. 'He had a wonderful power to win love from other men, yes, I use the word advisedly. It was not mere good-fellowship or even affection, but there was something so fine, so true, so strong and sweet in his nature, that it won the love of those who knew him best.' [13] The testimony of all these friends establishes his tenderness, his devotion, his loyalty. The long attachment of Aldrich, in particular, would do honor to any man. How charming is his brief account of the presence of his friend, with its suggestion of the link between them: 'Booth has been with us six weeks, acting wonderfully. We shall miss him sadly. He is a *great* actor. We love the boy. I like to mix his gloom with my sunshine.' [14]

In these familiar relations Booth dropped the reserve, the strange shyness that haunted him in larger gatherings. To be sure, even here he was not demonstrative, did not extend or seek gestures of affection with those he loved most. 'I never knew a man who had such an aversion to being caressed as he had,' says Mr. Bispham. 'He shrunk instinctively from any physical manifestation of personal affection, and while his friendships were strong, they were almost always unaccompanied by any outward demonstration save the grasp of the hand and the hearty welcome shining through his glorious eyes.' [15] But there was an even, kindly, sympathetic response, no temper, no petulance, no fretfulness. Those who knew him best found him always willing to give and take confidences. He loved a midnight talk by the latter end of a sea-coal fire and his complete naturalness gave such talk a singular intimate charm. 'There was something so magical, so mysterious, in his conversation that I gladly listened as long as he was willing to talk,' [16] writes Mr. Bispham. And again, 'We would talk so late that when we were ready to go to bed (we were never ready to stop talking), it was too late for me to go to my lodgings, and he would insist on my turning in with him.' [17]

In the even closer family circle Booth's affection is still more marked. He was devoted to his father while living and idolized his memory. His relation with his mother, who long survived her husband, was intimate and tender. He cared most faithfully and affectionately for his one daughter, the child of his first wife, and the daughter repaid him by a charming tribute after his death. The depth of their regard for each other is indicated by her with delicate and vivid tact: 'His nature was childlike, trustful, and dependent, yet he was always my wise and loving counsellor.' [18] And the father's testimony as to what his infant was to him is equally touching: 'She kept me happy while I was in Philadelphia, and is the light of my darkened life. All my hopes and aspirations now are clustering like a halo about my baby's head; to rear a monument to the mother in her child is my life-study now. I never had an aim or a hope before, and now my life is full of both.' [19]

To crown the analysis of Booth's personal history, one should consider the beauty and intensity of his brief first love. His second marriage connection, which lasted much longer, had some of the ups and downs and difficulties which are apt to attend human relations in this complicated world. The first was ideal and exquisite. The story of it should be read in the charming pages of Mrs. Aldrich, who saw it as intimately as any one. How great the wife's influence over her husband was is appreciated when we realize that the mere memory was sufficient to overcome permanently the inherited passion for alcohol which had earlier threatened to ravage his life. And his own beautiful words best indicate the depth and terror of the sense of loss which afflicted him: 'I call her, look for her, every time the door opens; in every car that passes our little cottage door, where we anticipated so much joy, I expect to see the loved form of her who was my *world*. God only can relieve me; nothing on earth can fill the place of her who was to me at once wife, mother, sister, child, guide, and savior. All is dark; I know not where to turn, how to direct the deserted vessel now.' [20]

II

It is not my business to discuss Booth's acting as such. I saw him only a few times, when I was too young to judge, and anyway my interest in the artist is only as he explains and illustrates the man. Of Booth's contemporaries most who were competent to speak rated his achievements highly. Now and then there is dissent, as moderately with Walt Whitman, who was always at least an independent judge. Whitman admired Booth's character, spoke of him as 'essentially a godlike man'; [21] but on the stage he found him inferior to his father, complained that he 'never made me forget everything else and follow him, as the greatest fellows, when they let themselves go, always do.' [22]

No one questions Booth's high, constant, and discerning personal devotion to his art. As to his influence upon its general history in America there is more difference of opinion. For ten years, from 1863 to 1873, he was concerned with the management of theaters and for four years he managed his own costly and superbly appointed house. His managerial skill and care are generally recognized. He engaged good actors, studied the details of production, and endeavored to make every point of the performance worthy of the greatest masterpieces of Shakespeare. One who watched him carefully and was competent to judge says of his management: 'No other "star," and I have seen many "stars" in that position, possessed his equanimity or displayed one tithe of his wonderful ability to direct.' [23] Mr. Winter insists, and justly, that Booth's object in this great undertaking was not financial profit. 'He sought to exalt the standard of dramatic art — not because he was specifically interested in the public welfare but because he was naturally prone to symmetry and loveliness of expression.' [24]

But the running of theaters is a business, and as a business man Booth was not a success. He had a simple trust in his fellows which was charming but fallacious. His theater was built in partnership and the handling of the finances was indiscreet. The result was failure and bankruptcy and Booth, after clearing himself honorably from the toils, never again attempted to be his own manager or to control his own surroundings. As a consequence, in later years he became apparently indifferent to where and with whom he acted. The companies that were engaged with him were too often mediocre and the scenery and properties were haphazard and neglected. 'He seems not even to have stipulated for decent competence in supporting players,' says Mr. Copeland, one of his most discriminating critics, 'or decent taste and liberality in the production.' [25] Mr. Winter's analysis of these vagaries is probably the correct one: 'He was a dreamer; and in every part of his life, as it was known to me during an intimacy extending over a period of about thirty years, I saw the operation of Hamlet's propensity to view all things as transitory and immaterial, and to let every thing drift. He was happier as an actor than as a manager.' [26] He himself wrote: 'I am a prime procrastinator and never (or "hardly ever") do to-day that which may be done to-morrow — or later.' [27]

But if Booth was sometimes careless as to what he felt to be outside his province, he was never slovenly or indifferent as regards his own personal art. He was indeed a creature of moods. Mr. Winter says that his performances of even his best parts were unequal.[28] Sometimes the occasion, the circumstances, the audience roused him and he burst out into transcendent brilliancy. At other times his work was careful, thoughtful, but uninspired. It is curious to have his own testimony that to feel the part too keenly himself was not always conducive to making others feel it. Once when acting 'The Fool's Revenge' he was moved to tears and thought that he had been unusually successful. His daughter said to him afterwards, 'What was the matter with you to-night, father? I never saw you give such a poor performance of the part.' [29]

But, whether inspiration came or not, he was always the conscientious, self-respecting artist, determined to give the very best that was in him and to interpret the works of great poets with every atom of his natural intelligence and power. He did not perhaps reflect abstractly and metaphysically on the nature of acting so much as some others, though there is most curious matter in his brief analysis of the acting of Kean.[30] But his patience in minute study of his own parts and plays was unfailing, inexhaustible. 'There was not a line in any of his Shakespearean plays,' says Mr. Winter, 'that he had not studiously and thoroughly considered; not a vexed point that he had not scanned; not a questionable reading that he had not, for his own purposes in acting, satisfactorily settled.'[31] So with stage business. He knew the methods of those who had preceded him, and employed them when he saw fit, and again he was endlessly ingenious in inventing novel and effective devices of his own. Nor was his study of the plays confined to his own part. His correspondence with Mr. Furness as to various Shakespearean puzzles and characters is as illuminating as it is modest and unpretentious.

And his art grew and developed to the end. As a young man, he naturally copied to some extent the rougher, bolder style of his father, which in his father's hands had been so effective. But besides the desire to be original and independent, he soon came to feel that his temperament and artistic instincts were different from his father's. He dropped some of the more violent parts, like Sir Giles Overreach, and into all he introduced more thoughtfulness, more sensibility, more of the high imaginative quality, the poetry, which made his Hamlet so peculiarly fascinating. His own account of the intelligent effort involved in shaking off the imitation of his father is of extreme interest: 'It took me several years to rid myself of this fault; all my father's mannerisms and imperfections I acquired by being so constantly with him. When they were pointed out to me, I watched myself closely and rooted them out.' [32]

One misconception which sprang from Booth's so frequently appearing with inferior actors should be finally disposed of: the calumny that he shrank from comparison and rivalry with his equals. It seems to be beyond dispute that he was at all times free from the professional jealousy which is popularly supposed to be one of the evils of stage life. 'I never knew an actor whose mind was more free than that of Booth from envy and bitterness,' says Mr. Winter. 'The prosperity of other actors gave him pleasure, and their adversity gave him pain.' [33] When he commented on the performance of others, it was manifestly in a vein of abstract criticism and always in the spirit which he so charmingly commends to his daughter: 'Bear charity in your thoughts, love in your heart, for all.

"Still in thy right hand carry gentle peace,
To silence envious tongues,"

says Shakespeare, who says scarcely anything that is not true and good.' [34]

Even more substantial evidence of Booth's large-mindedness is the fact that he acted at one time or another with nearly all the best actors of his generation, Irving, Salvini, Charlotte Cushman, Janauschek, Barrett, Modjeska. It seems unlikely that any other actor ever coöperated so extensively and, what is most significant of all, Mr. Copeland records that two of these distinguished persons told him 'that they found Booth's courtesy almost unexampled.' [35]

It is true that his sense of humor could not always resist the pretensions of those who thought themselves excellent, but were not. 'Great actors,' he writes ironically, 'are very queer cusses to handle; besides there are so many of 'em. Nearly every company counts a dozen such.' [36] It must not, however, be supposed from this that he was scornful of his humbler companions or tactless in dealing with them. On the contrary, nothing shows more the essential fineness of his nature than the considerate and gentle manner in which he treated even the lowest subordinates about the theater. He was quiet and unobtrusive as to his own comfort and accommodations. 'I have frequently seen him during a performance, while waiting for his cue, walk across to his dressing-room and bring out a chair for himself rather than ask any one else to do it,' says Mr. Malone.[37] If suggestion or correction were needed, he attended to it in private if possible, or if in public, with some touch of humor or sympathetic understanding that made reproof comfortable to receive and easy to profit by. Shy as he was in general society, his fellow actors who traveled with him, found him companionable and helpful. When they were all on the road together, 'after a time his timidity disappeared and he was like the father of a big family.'[38] He told charming stories of his past experience and made himself instructive and entertaining both. Yet with all his gentleness, his discipline and control during his brief period of management were such as to attract the highest praise from those best qualified to judge. Jefferson. said, 'Booth's theater is conducted as a theater should be — like a church behind the curtain and like a counting-house in front of it.'[39] And Boucicault's comment was, 'I have been in every theater I think in civilized Christendom, and Booth's is the only theater that I have seen properly managed.' [40] Booth's own idea of the morals of the matter is well illustrated by his stern reply to a minister who wrote to ask if there was not some private door by which he could enter unobserved: 'There is no door in my theater through which God cannot see.' [41]

Though, on the whole, Booth's professional career was remarkably smooth and successful, he had his times of struggle, trial, and discouragement. The bohemian wandering of his earlier days cannot have been especially attractive to his domestic, quiet temperament, even in youth. As he grew older, he resented it bitterly. He wanted a home, a calm abiding-place, with books and friends and love about him, such a refuge as he at last established in a measure at the Players Club. Instead, he was hustled from one place to another, from one world to another. Hotels were wretched, food was unpalatable, life in railroad trains was agitating and dirty and wearisome. He could not read, he could not think, he could not rest. 'What a miserable existence is the actor's, especially if he is domestically inclined! Home is something denied to him.' [42]

The financial failure of his theater would have been a serious blow to any man. But Booth took it with such courage and dignity as made it seem slighter than it was. Then there was criticism, which probably descends more brutally and more stupidly upon the actor than upon any one else. Booth sometimes made light of it and sometimes profited by it, but of course at times it hurt. In the main, however, he overlooked it and avoided it, especially when it took the gossipy and personal form. 'I care so little for theatrical notices or news "puffery,"' he wrote, 'that I seldom read them.' ⁴³ And again, 'I have long since ceased to read "theatrical news," and have succeeded in letting my "dear friends" know that I avoid such rot, and that it is brutal to mention it to me. I repeat to them the remark Howells made to Aldrich when Aldrich asked him if he had heard of some abuse of his (Howells's) writings: "Do you suppose that I have no bosom friends?"' ⁴⁴

Through all these petty annoyances and greater difficulties there was the firm determination to succeed, or at any rate to deserve success. Booth's quiet, unpretentious manner and reluctance to talk of his aims or his triumphs made him seem indifferent. He certainly cared less than some about cheap notoriety. The curious gaze of idle gapers is, he, says, 'unpleasant for me, who hate notoriety and publicity.' 45 And some have extended this into an inference that he lacked ambition and really cared little about his artistic career. But if you read his letters closely, you see that to accomplish what he had struggled for all his life meant something to him, as it does to others. Does not ambition speak right out in this striking passage, written in 1865? 'The terrible success of "Hamlet" seems to swallow up everything else theatrical, and the desire I have to follow it up with something still better done, if it can be, in the way of costumes and scenery, keeps me far off in fairy-land, day and night, in my dreams and in my days (if I can't say waking hours), and time flies unheeded by me.' 46 An even more rapturous note is heard in 1883, after the magnificent reception in Germany: 'I have just accomplished the one great object of my professional aspiration. . . . This is the realization of my twenty years' dream. . . . I cannot tell you of my triumph to-night without a gush of egotism — and you know how difficult that is for me.' 47

It was difficult, and if we would learn of his triumphs, we have to do it usually from others. But it may be said in general that he won applause, commendation, and popularity from the very beginning of his career and retained them and increased them until the end. Something in his very aspect, the grace of his movement, the thoughtful beauty of his countenance, the fire of his eye, the magic of his diction, seemed to charm men — and women — and dispose them to regard his every effort favorably. 'When he walked in the streets of Boston in 1857,' says Mr. Winter, 'his shining face, his compact figure, and his elastic step drew every eye, and people would pause and turn in groups to look at him.' [48] It was so everywhere. Few actors can boast more unanimity of affectionate admiration. I do not know that I can sum this up better than by quoting again his own words, with their charming turn of modesty, as to the reception in Germany which delighted him so much: 'Oh, I wish you had been present to-night! When I am cooler I will try to give you a full account of the night's work. The actors as well as the audience were very enthusiastic, many of the former kissing my hands and thanking me over and over again — for what I know not, unless because they recognized in me a sincere disciple of their idol Shakespeare.' [49]

Yet all this flood of glory brought the recipient of

it little satisfaction. It was not that he was discontented, or yearned for greater triumphs or wider victory. But his temperament was such that he felt the emptiness of success, the hollowness of the triumphs of the world. Hard as he toiled at his own profession, he did not esteem it among the highest. 'Very great writers,' he said, 'may stand full length among the statesmen and warriors, but as a rule, they, with artists, especially actors, should be permitted only an occasional bust in some quiet corner.' [50] And it was not the actor's glory only, but renown and public admiration of every kind that seemed to him in many aspects irksome and almost hateful. 'They point at me and touch me, exclaiming to one another, "That's him!" "That's Booth!" . . . I suppose they mean it all in kindness, but it is very disagreeable.' [51] 'Never was there an actor who had such an extravagant following of adulation — never one to whom, apparently, it was so indifferent,' says Mrs. Aldrich.[52] He himself spoke of the years following his visit to Germany as 'tediously successful.' [53] And in his sympathetic and profound memoir of his father he says of him, in words that are equally appropriate to the son: 'Indeed, he ever seemed to muse with Omar Khayyam thus:

AS GOD MADE THEM

"The worldly hope men set their hearts upon
Turns ashes — or it prospers; and anon,
Like snow upon the desert's dusty face,
Lighting a little hour or two — is gone."' [54]

III

For at the bottom of the man's heart, no matter what fame beguiled him or what outward activity might tempt him, there was a taint of brooding melancholy, a sense of the dreary unreality of life, which no glory of success, no amusement or distraction could wholly banish. 'This is about all I know,' he writes, 'beyond the limit of my fancy world, where I dream my life away.' [55] And the dreams were mostly far from being rose-color.

Not that he indulged in maudlin pessimism, or developed this tendency in himself in any morbid fashion. On the contrary, it is most interesting to watch the various devices he employed to escape from the demon that haunted him. Even the most seductive one to a weak nature, the resort to stimulants, for a time had an inherited hold on him. And the hints we get of his battle with it add to his charm. In a profoundly pathetic sentence he writes to his daughter: 'Much of my life's struggle has been with myself, and the pain I have endured in overcoming and correcting the evils of my untrained disposition has been very great.' [56] He could at times speak of the struggle lightly, as when he remarked to Charles Barron, after a performance of 'Othello,' 'Oh, Charley, my boy, there's no use talking. This part is a great provocation to drink.' [57] But a very different aspect of it appears in the words quoted by Mrs. Aldrich: 'No one can imagine the call of that desire. When it engulfs me, I could sell my soul, my hope of salvation, for just one glass.' [58] From the refuge of drugged oblivion, a remedy far worse than the disease of melancholy, strong love saved him.

We have already seen the relief Booth found from his tendency to brooding in laborious devotion to his art and in affectionate intercourse with those who loved him. As regards the latter, it should be insisted that he did not intrude his own sadness upon others, never went about with the affectation of a long face and a settled gloom. He objected particularly to being considered 'Hamlety' in private life, and he was not so.[59] On the contrary, he had a quick sense of fun, could take a joke and make one. Sometimes, indeed, his practical jesting was of a rather grim order, as when he had the bullet, fired at him by an assassin, mounted in gold and inscribed, 'From Mark Gray *to* Edwin

Booth.' [60] But he could pass a bright and gay retort, like that to Sothern, who once remarked, 'The worst performance ever seen was my Armand Duval.' To which Booth replied, 'The worst? Did you ever see my Romeo?' [61] He could tell a story admirably, with endless resources of effective mimicry. And the stories of others sometimes moved him to laughter so extreme that it caused real physical pain.[62] Yet even in the laughter and merriment there was apt to be a suggestion, which Mr. Greenslet has well characterized in speaking of Booth's letters to Aldrich, 'with their undertone of tragic gloom, their pathetic eagerness for affection and mirth.' [63] And the study of many of Booth's letters is extremely interesting from this point of view. It is said that he never succeeded on the stage in a really comic part. So with the letters. They are often playful, often touched with a quaint and delicate fancy that is exceedingly winning. It can never be said that there is anything forced or artificial about their gayety. Yet they rarely make you laugh, or even smile. They do not have the irresistible fun which gleams and dances through the correspondence of Lamb or that of Cowper, both, by the way, exceedingly melancholy persons when the mood came upon them.

EDWIN BOOTH

As Booth found refuge from his sadness in work and in friendship, so he sought it in other forms of spiritual exaltation. With his fine sensibility to all sorts of influences, he must have been peculiarly susceptible to beauty in every shape. Yet I do not find much reference to the general enjoyment of art, perhaps because his professional occupations were themselves of such an essentially artistic nature. He loved music and in his youth was a not inexpert performer. He appreciated Nature, as appears in an occasional vivid touch: 'I'm passionately fond of trees, especially when near the water.' [64] Above all, the lofty splendor of Shakespearean poetry had become interwoven with the whole texture of his spirit, though perhaps this involved as much suggestion of sorrow as of joy. And it is curious to see how the tainted, darkened view creeps into even the possible fruition of what is beautiful: 'It is nearly always my fate to miss the beauties of travel, and to be prevented from enjoying the places I visit through some mischance.' [65]

With intellectual resources Booth was more or less conversant outside of his thorough study for his own work. He had little education as a boy and deplores it: 'How often, oh! how often have I imagined the delights of a collegiate education!

What a world of never-ending interest lies open
to the master of languages!' [66] But his reading,
though erratic, was fairly wide, and he could reflect
deeply when a subject interested him. The studies
that he wrote of his father and of Edmund Kean
show remarkable originality and insight, as compared, for instance, with much of the critical
writing about Booth himself. At the same time, I
have not felt him generally to be a profound thinker
and it is noticeable that his peculiar melancholy
does not connect itself in the least degree with the
great romantic types which were popular in his day.
So far as his recognition of them is concerned,
Rousseau, René, Byron, Shelley, George Sand,
Obermann, might never have existed.

That is to say, the sadness from which Booth
suffered was not rooted in any intellectual skepti-
cism, or theoretical disbelief in the moral and provi-
dential government of the world. Even the agony
of loss could wring from him only a momentary
question: 'A terrible nightmare, *doubt*, will thrust
itself between me and heaven, and my mind is on
the rack.' [67] At times his faith went so far as actual
spiritualism and a decided interest in direct communication with the dead.[68] But in the main it was
a large, simple belief in the pervading and reassur-

ing goodness of God. 'Believe in one great truth, Ad. — God is. And as surely as you and I are flesh and bones and blood, so are we also spirits eternal.' [69] Evil might be haunting, encroaching, involving. Life might perplex, torment, above all might weary unspeakably. But some day we should read the riddle of it: 'Let it pass; life is a great big spelling-book, and on every page we turn, the words grow harder to understand the meaning of. But there *is* a meaning, and when the last leaf flops over, we'll know the whole lesson by heart.' [70]

Yet, in spite of the value of even this highest refuge of all, the weight of sadness was there, and constant, and permanent. No doubt in Booth's case the tragic accumulation of external circumstance immensely increased it. His father, to whom he lived in peculiar nearness, was snatched from him at an early age. His young wife was torn away after a few months of what seemed almost perfect felicity. Just as he was beginning to recover from this, his brother's terrible crime threatened to blight his whole career and did blight his heart. His greatest professional effort ended in financial ruin. The death of his second wife involved extreme distress. And toward the end illness developed his prevailing depression to peculiar intensity.

AS GOD MADE THEM

The patience and self-control with which Booth
endured all these afflictions are not the least attractive features of his character. They certainly
justified his choice of the words of Hamlet for his
epitaph: [71]

> 'Thou hast been
> As one, in suffering all, that suffers nothing,
> A man that Fortune's buffets and rewards
> Hast ta'en with equal thanks.'

Nay, more, he believed that the evil must turn to
good, and that somewhere, somehow, the discipline
of sorrow would enure to benefit: '"I have looked
upon the world for (nearly double) four times
seven years, and since I could distinguish" good
from bad, I have regarded what men term misfor-
tune as the best tonic an apathetic spirit can receive.' [72] And he had further that strange inocula-
tion for suffering which is the doubtful privilege of
those who perpetually conjure up imaginary evils:
'All my life has been passed on "picket duty," as it
were. I have been on guard, on the lookout for dis-
asters — for which, when they come, I am prepared. Therefore, I have seemed, to those who do
not really know me, callous to the many blows that
have been dealt me.' [73] Yet with all this it will be
admitted that he had trials enough to shake the

firm poise of any man. The mountain pressure of them might well account for any sorrow and no doubt they did greatly augment the sadness of Booth's later years.

At the same time, we must conclude that they did not cause it, that there was something fundamental, temperamental, that tainted his soul early and late. It is true, he himself said: 'I was always of a boyish spirit, and if my physical health were good, I should still be very boyish; but there was always an air of melancholy about me, that made me seem much more serious than I ever really was.' [74] Nevertheless, Mr. Winter's sentence on his boyhood must be accepted as summing up substantial evidence: 'As a boy, he was grave, observant, thoughtful, appreciative of his surroundings, and especially reticent.' [75] In the letters of even his early years we get glimpses of the prevailing disposition: 'Surely I ought to be happy — yet I cannot say I am so. Only look at my case. Here have I been traveling since childhood almost, without a home. I have been longing for these summer months, that I might pass them in quiet with my family — but, lo! in a few weeks I must trudge again.' [76] And to this we must add his own terrible phrase, that he 'never knew a really happy day.' [77]

Some strange, vague inheritance, some mysterious affliction, infection, haunted his footsteps always, as those of so many others, and tinged even felic-ity with the brooding shadow of despair. Let the psycho-analysts probe the secret. We can only register it as established beyond all possibility of question. For external evidence, which swarms on every hand, we need no more than the brief sentence of Mr. Copeland: 'I thought then that I had never seen so sad a face, and I have never yet beheld a sadder one.' [78] As to Booth's own testimony, the abundance of it makes selection difficult. 'For God's reward for what I have done, I can hardly appreciate it; 'tis more like a punishment for misdeeds (of which I've done many) than grace for good ones (if I've done any).' [79] Life he calls 'this hell of misery to which we have been doomed.' [80] And he 'cannot grieve at death. It seems to me the greatest boon the Almighty has granted us.' [81] Again, 'Why do not you look at this miserable little life, with all its ups and downs, as I do? At the very worst, 'tis but a scratch, a temporary ill, to be soon cured, by that dear old doctor, Death — who gives us a life more healthful and enduring than all the physicians, temporal or spiritual, can give.' [82]

I have sometimes wondered how far this spirit

of melancholy brooding in Booth was fostered by living from childhood in the lives of others, by too wide a spiritual roving in the mysterious world of other men's souls. This is not always the effect, and it is in some artists entirely different. But given Booth's temper, the intimate association with imaginary figures, especially those racked by overwhelming sorrows, must necessarily have deepened the detachment and heightened the gloom. Above all must this have been the case in such a long and close identification with Hamlet, the prime embodiment of the reflective sorrow of the world. Yet even here we cannot help feeling that, much as Booth may have been influenced by Hamlet's character, his supreme success in the part sprang from his own instinctive and inborn sympathy with it. His unfortunate brother seized the truth admirably when he said, 'No! no, no! There's but one Hamlet to my mind, that's my brother Edwin. You see, between ourselves, he *is* Hamlet, melancholy and all.' [83]

There is one other Shakespearean figure who seems to express much of Booth's temperament, and that is the Jaques of 'As You Like It.' I cannot discover that Booth ever acted Jaques, but I should like immensely to have seen him do it.

AS GOD MADE THEM

Would he not have found something of his own
soul in this dreamer who has discovered 'a melancholy of mine own, compounded of many simples,
extracted from many objects; and indeed the
sundry contemplation of my travels, in which my
often rumination wraps me in a most humorous
sadness'? [84] Would not he who had fed his spirit
for fifty years on the music of the great poets
have echoed with passion Jaques's whimsical complaint, 'I can suck melancholy out of a song as a
weasel sucks eggs'? [85]

But if Jaques had Hamlet's melancholy, he had
not his charm. Booth had, and it drew all men and
women to him, and draws us even to-day, who read
of him in old and dusty books. A strangely subtle,
winning grace lingers about his memory and we
can well understand the love and grief that breathe
through Aldrich's description of the final parting
at Mount Auburn: 'There in the tender afterglow
two or three hundred men and women stood silent,
with bowed heads. A single bird, in a nest hidden
somewhere near by, twittered from time to time.
The soft June air, blowing across the upland,
brought with it the scent of syringa blossoms from
the slope below. Overhead and among the trees
the twilight was gathering. "Good-night, sweet

Prince!" I said, under my breath. . . . Then I thought of the years and years that had been made rich with his presence, and of the years that were to come, . . . and if there had not been a crowd of people, I would have buried my face in the greensward and wept, as men may not do, and women may. And thus we left him.' [86]

VI
PORTRAIT OF A SCHOLAR
FRANCIS JAMES CHILD

CHRONOLOGY

FRANCIS JAMES CHILD

Born, Boston, February 1, 1825.
Graduated, Harvard, 1846.
In Europe, 1849–1851.
Professor of Rhetoric, Harvard, 1851.
Edition of Spenser published, 1855.
Early edition of Ballads published, 1857.
Married Elizabeth Sedgwick, August 23, 1860.
Observations on Chaucer published, 1863.
Professor of English, Harvard, 1876.
Final edition of Ballads begun, 1882.
Died, Boston, September 11, 1896.

FRANCIS JAMES CHILD

FRANCIS JAMES CHILD

I

THROUGH the second half of the nineteenth century, Francis James Child lived a quiet scholar's life in Cambridge. Vast and conscientious work, old songs, dreams, and roses made up the whole of it. He had friends whom he adored; he had pupils for whom he labored faithfully and whom he sent out into the wide world with a message of devotion to ideals, of high and unfailing purpose, of faith in joy, in beauty, and in God. Such messages get no large publicity, they are not heralded with drums and trumpets; but they travel far and sink deep into the hearts that are suited to them, and they are not forgotten.

Professor Child will be chiefly remembered for his thorough, profound, and probably final work on the old English ballads. To be sure, he himself would have been the first to insist that no scholarly work could be really final; yet there are few to whom his own admirable saying, 'Do it so it shall never have to be done again,' [1] would be more perfectly applicable. The immense research, not only into all possible English and Scottish sources, both

oral and manuscript, but into the comparative folk-
lore and legend of the Continental languages, was
no more remarkable than the tact and unerring instinct which distinguished the true from the false
and separated what was enduringly human from
what was pretentiously literary. Professor Kittredge — and no man living is more competent to
judge — declares that 'as an investigator Professor
Child was at once the inspiration and the despair of
his disciples. Nothing could surpass the scientific
exactness of his methods and the unwearied dili-
gence with which he conducted his researches.' [2]
Yet at the same time what mainly touched and interested him in all the mass of archæological fact
was the human heart, 'that universal humanity
which always moved him, wherever he found it,
whether in the pages of a mediæval chronicle, or in
the stammering accents of a late and vulgarly distorted ballad, or in the faces of the street boys who
begged roses from his garden.' [3]

And this vast effort of research was pursued side
by side with a round of college duties which many
men would have deemed sufficient occupation for
an ordinary life. Correspondence was carried on
with scholars all over the world. Time had to be
made, had to be snatched, had to be stolen. 'He

FRANCIS JAMES CHILD

was reminded ... of the paucity of materials, and particularly of the slender margin of leisure which had been at his disposal for original work. "Yes," he assented, as he stood by the fireplace, "I hadn't much time for it; but I kept the books and papers ready on my desk, and sat down to them, even if there were only twenty minutes or so free."' 4 In his light and casual way he could make fun of all the labor, 'procrastination, a vice, which I find by practice to be as bad as it is said to be in the copy-books,' 5 but few men have overcome procrastination by sterner habit of routine. Above all, he understood the distinction, so difficult to make in his line of work, between a distracted over-conscientiousness, which vainly torments itself, and a frivolous disregard of exactitude. How many scholars might profit by his maxim, so simply expressed to Lowell, 'I must not be careless, but must still less be fussy.' 6 For fussiness has ruined some of the best work of the world.

It must not be supposed that great results were achieved in this case, any more than in others, without difficulties and rebuffs and failures and discouragements. There were times when things went well and times when they did not. 'I work now every day on this material, and sometimes am in

good spirits about it and sometimes very low.' [7]
There were the endless interruptions, interruptions
of necessary duty, attended to with cheerfulness,
but taking time and strength, interruptions of unnecessary bores, who wasted a day with tedious
chat and dissipated precious hours when what at
least seemed worthy things might have been accomplished. There was the inevitable doom, always treading on the heels of accomplishment and
threatening to snatch it away: 'I have had another
panic about not living to see the end of the thing,
and have been like the hermit in the desert who is
running from death. The only way to get on is to
work doggedly through dull and pleasant alike, and
just now the work is dull.' [8]

Also, there were the external discouragements,
the flaunt of false scholarship, the blare of insincere
publicity. There was the apparent trend of education away from the things of the spirit to the material, the expedient, the so-called practical, which
took more account of body than of soul. To all
these annoyances Child was in a sense indifferent,
nobly indifferent. 'The most grotesque distortions,
spread abroad as fresh conquests of truth, by the
great army [of notoriety seekers], drew from him no
more than his favorite comment, "Let the children

play.'" [9] Yet there were moments when such things fretted and depressed.

But, on the whole, the work was full of delight, as varied as it was absorbing; and the worker asked nothing better than to give his life to it. 'His life and his learning were one; his work was the expression of himself,' says Professor Kittredge, admirably.[10] There was the delight of discovery, the long, dull grind for days of slow turning over of dusty folios, and then the sudden surprise of coming across some bit of grace and freshness, some revelation of music or color, such pleasure as gleams through the comment on a Scandinavian folk-song, 'It is a jewel that any clime might envy.' [11] There was always that keen, quick sense of humanity, the manifold sympathy with human nature, which is so often lacking to great scholarship, but which was ever present in Child and never failing, ready at any moment to detect the natural touch under archaic disguises and the quaint stiffness of the traditional phrase.

It was this intense human instinct which made his public lectures and readings so delightful and popular. He took the old texts and put life into them as the author might have done himself. Hear what Lowell says of his reading of Chaucer: 'He wound into the meaning of it (as Doctor Johnson says of Burke) like a serpent, or perhaps I should come nearer to it if I said that he injected the veins of the poem with his own sympathetic humor, till it seemed to live again. I could see his hearers take the fun before it came, the faces lighting with the reflection of his.' [12]

The same fresh and natural human grace touches and colors the introductions and notes of the great edition of the 'Ballads' and makes them alive. Songs that might seem quaint and stiff in their dialectic garb, might fail to stir and move us merely from their secular remoteness, somehow acquire vigor and vitality under his touch, seem to be dealing with scenes and persons, at any rate with passions, such as are flowing and fighting about us daily. The vast erudition involved in the scholar's researches shows itself without a shade of pedantry, because it is not taken too seriously, is served up to us in a delicate, playful vein, which proves at once that the caterer understood the fragility as well as the profound human truth of the eternal trifles he was dealing with. A few illustrations here and there will hardly suffice to convey the charming tone of the whole. But how tender is the reference to 'the beautiful fancy of plants springing from the graves of star-crossed lovers, and signifying by the intertwining of stems or leaves, or in other analogous ways, that an earthly passion has not been extinguished by death.' [13] How dainty is the play of whimsical humor in the comment: 'They cast lots, and the lot falls on Annie — a result which strikes us as having more semblance of the "corrupted currents of this world" than of a pure judgment of God'; [14] or in this other, 'The phrase looks more malicious than *naïf* . . . and implies, I fear, an exsufflicate and blown surmise about female virtue.' [15] While there is an enchanting hint of fun in the remark as to the legendary danger of kissing one's love in hell: 'How the lover escaped in this instance is not explained. Such things happen sometimes, but not often enough to encourage one to take the risk.' [16]

When one appreciates this gift of apt and delicate expression, one is tempted to regret that Child did not do more original writing. The grace and wit of his letters alone would suffice to prove that he might have done far more for the world in this way than he actually did. But any desire for general literary fame was restrained by the charming innate modesty which was so conspicuous in him always and which shows in the earnest request to Lowell:

'I wish you would *alter the note* [of compliment] and strike out on page 160 "who has done more," etc. I am content to have "fittingly" remain, if you think it should, but that is quite flattery enough for me.' [17]

He asked no more than to do his own chosen work faithfully and in a manner to gain the respect of his colleagues and the attachment of those who came under his instruction. It is needless to point out that in both these points he was successful in the highest degree. Those who collaborated with him for years on the college faculty bear unanimous witness to his sincerity, his fidelity, his devoted industry, his self-forgetful and self-sacrificing public spirit. His temper was quick and his opinions positive and vividly expressed; but hasty words were regretted as soon as uttered. How pretty is the picture of a sharp battle of arguments between him and Shaler, whose tongue was as nimble and whose heart was as tender as his, followed immediately after the return home by a swift exchange of apologetic and remorseful notes. [18] How touching is the tribute of Barrett Wendell to the older teacher, whose attitude toward life and literature was in many respects so different: 'The academic leader, whose seniority alone were enough to have warranted unquestioning precedence, was not only a scholar and a teacher whose name was known wherever our language is studied, but he was also a friend on whose kindness, despite all divergency of theories and methods, they might confidently depend.' [19] The weary and preoccupied searcher was ready at any moment to lay aside his own pursuits and give his time and thought to helping his friends or even those who had little or no claim upon him. When Gummere parted from him, after a pleasant social hour, Child said earnestly, of a great but unjustly treated scholar who had been with them, 'Ah, but we must do something for that man.' And Gummere remarks, 'These were the last words I heard him say, and they were characteristic of all I had ever heard from him, of all I had ever heard about him.' [20]

Child's relations with his pupils were as cordial and as profitable as with his colleagues and fellow-workers. It is true that he was not over-patient with indolence or indifference and that he was prone to prick the bubble of pretentious vanity wherever he found it. No man could impose on him and, modest and unpretentious as he was, he was quite able on occasion to assert his dignity and self-respect. How excellent is Gummere's account of the student who began to give a pompous and rhetorical reading of 'Hamlet'! 'Mr. Child uncoiled himself slowly, craned out his head, lifted his spectacles, and peered, first amazed, then quizzical, then tragic, at the performer: "Heavens! man — stop!"' [21] How vivid is the story of the costly English copy of Chaucer which was sent flying through the classroom window, because the editor had ventured to Bowdlerize the old poet's vigorous and manly phraseology.[22]

But there is general agreement of all those worthy to judge as to the immense, infectious stimulus of Child's love and enthusiasm for what was rare and beautiful. The quiet, thoughtful scholar imparted his own delight to those who were able to appreciate it, and they went forth and diffused it all over the country and all over the world. And as he was ready to inspire, so he was ready to help. He would give his time, his thought, his limited means to any student who really showed the ability, or even the disposition to profit by them. 'One thing may be safely asserted,' says Mr. Kittredge; 'no university teacher was ever more beloved.' [23] And an old pupil puts the same thing even more strikingly: 'His influence was more powerful, because it was subtle, and although he does not seem to be well known, I have met men in many parts of the world who immediately fell on my neck when I said I had been a pupil of "Stubby Child." [24]

II

Nor must it be for a moment supposed that Child's relations and connections were limited to academic surroundings and to those who had a part in his scholarly pursuits. He was a man of the world and knew the world, and all its subtle, winding ways, even while he kept himself unspotted from it. He enjoyed the diversions of men, the common, simple ones, the diversions of children, enjoyed them as a child. He enjoyed the circus, and was a frequenter of Barnum's. He and Lowell 'enjoyed a charming bear, who visited us at Elmwood the last time I was with him, as much as any of the other children.' [25]

He entered with even more zest into public, serious pursuits, and perhaps was not incapable of finding them more diverting than the circuses. He threw all the ardor of his intense and sensitive nature into political thought and discussion, and his love for democracy, in the highest sense, was as eager as his love for Shakespeare and old ballads. Especially he resented wrong and cruelty and injustice. 'When he was confronted with injury or oppression,' says Professor Kittredge, 'none could stand against the anger of this just man. His unselfishness did not suffer him to see offences against himself, but wrong done to another aroused him in an instant to protesting action.' [26] It was this ardor which sustained his hope and enthusiasm through all the bitter years of the Civil War. In spite of his age, he himself would have fought, if physical strength had permitted it. But all that an earnest tongue and pen and unremitting effort could do to support the national cause was done from the beginning to the end. Even in so remote a place as the introductions to the ballads, the wide passion for justice found a chance to assert itself: 'And these pretended child-murders with their horrible consequences, are only a part of a persecution [of the Jews], which, with all moderation, may be rubricated as the most disgraceful chapter in the history of the human race.' [27]

This political activity was not confined to larger issues. Child would omit his classes to go and distribute ballots at the polls. He would attend caucuses and political meetings, and speak, if necessary. He would oppose the local boss with a vehemence that made friends gather about after the meeting in dread of actual conflict. Yet the vehemence was tempered with such evident sincerity and fundamental human kindness that the boss walked up and offered a cigar, instead of a threat. And Child accepted the cigar, with the remark: 'I can match you in any of your *little* vices.' [28]

The fundamental human kindness was neverfailing, affecting friend and foe, rich and poor, inmate and stranger, with equal warmth and equal sunny charity. He would give his time to studying needs and his moderate resources to relieving them. For his resources were moderate. The salary of a professor hardly went further in those days than now for meeting the varied requirements of a family, for keeping up the tone of social life in a semiurban atmosphere, and for purchasing the many books and accessories indispensable for the scholar's wide and original research. There is no complaint of the limits: on the contrary, always a humorous acceptance of them. But one gets an occasional glimpse of how narrow they were: 'Were it not for the pay — small as it is — I should certainly stop after the third course. I *must* earn eight or ten hundreds extra for the present; but the consequences look bad — nothing else done and no real vacation.' [29]

Yet, no matter how moderate the resources, there was always something for the need of those who were more limited still. All who knew Child well insist upon the amplitude of his beneficence and his constant readiness to respond to appeals for charity of all kinds. Indeed, his unfailing tenderness and sympathy made him liable to be easily imposed upon and this would have amounted almost to a weakness, if it had not been for the sense of humor which made him the first to appreciate the comic facility with which he was taken in. Hear him tell the story of one experience: 'That is the point of the diurnal revolution where I am, just after receiving a second call from a discharged convict, who finds it difficult to get back to a respectable career, a pretty tough problem for him and for me. Having had to do with two or three of these fellows, I am likely to have a very fair *clientèle*. . . . It is wonderful, what decent-looking fellows some of them are, by nature; or is it that I am not a connoisseur?' [30]

In more normal social relations with humanity, Child was generally responsive and always attractive. It is true that he was by nature shy and self-effacing. One of his colleagues tells of the amusement of seeing a pompous minor official stride across the Yard, forcing everybody out of his way, while little 'Stubby' Child trotted along with his bag of books, turning out for even an insignificant freshman. Also, he had the busy man's hatred of those who have no use for their time except to devour other people's. 'There is no escape from them. I bow my head meekly, not always so very meekly, there are maledictions when the door opens, but I yield, give forced attention, hope that they will go, see them rise with a sigh of relief, see them sit again with a sigh of despair — well, probably I have my allowance for to-day.' [31] And he had the simple, unconventional man's, or why not say, the man's, hatred of formality, and dinner-clothes, and those little elements of the parade of life so sacred to the feminine heart. 'A dinner-party for six or seven (the hosts being in formal mourning, which keeps the tone agreeably low, and the movement *allegro, ma non troppo*) would certainly be a good thing twice a week, were I sufficiently civilized, and I think I could submit to be civilized enough, if I could go without heart-eating cares.' [32]

But when he once submitted to the dinner-clothes, and still more, when the dinner-clothes were not required and there was informal and un-ushered ease, he was sure to enjoy himself, and others were sure to enjoy themselves, at any rate. There was a charm about his appearance, the shrewd, homely, kindly, responsive face, set in its frame of auburn curls. There was a charm about his soul, a kindly, homely, engaging naturalness, which put the shyest at their ease and drew wit or comprehension from the dryest and dullest. He loved children and was a child with them and with their elders, so that Howells plays delightfully upon the aptness of his name.[33] It is really surprising how universal is the agreement among all sorts of persons as to this pervading charm, so that Henry and William James, Doctor Hale, Howells, Norton, and a dozen others repeat some such words as Lowell's: 'Child goes on winning all ears and all hearts.' [34]

There was something gay and sprightly about his spirit, with all its refinement and reserve, something of the waywardness and elfishness of the old songs he so greatly loved, which sometimes showed in odd and playful freaks, as when with his three little girls he performed the ballad of 'Young Beichan' at a Christmas entertainment,[35] or united with Lowell in the lyrical frolic of the 'Pesceballo.' And again, the spirit flowed out in the infinite humor of his letters, sometimes in wild puns, worthy of the most licentious extravagance of Lamb, sometimes in rollicking exaggeration, as on the staid, conservative diversions of ancient Boston: 'Nevertheless, in far-off Madrid, cold perhaps, shady probably, foreign altogether, even an *Advertiser* must have a fairly agreeable taste — the advertisements are there; some of them are new too, but you could find India Wharf and Long Wharf, and *horse sales* — don't you like those? The horse not afraid of anything — not afraid of ——? Raciness in the *Advertiser* remains only in the horse columns. Have you noticed how the fellows that write fireworks ads are going out, perhaps gone out? Had Boston known what was for its peace, it would always keep the fourth of July show for the genius that the institution fostered. It was fully equal to Sir Thomas Mallory. Now a race has come that knows not Jacob — Boston is not Boston.' [36] Could the soul of Lamb flicker and trifle more deliciously?

With this social grace and attraction, and with the deeper qualities beyond it, it is unnecessary to say that Child was beloved. He was not so widely known as some, though the circle of even his intimate acquaintance was fairly large. But in that circle he is invariably spoken of with a peculiar tenderness. And the tenderness was amply merited by the warmth of affection which went out from him to meet it. 'He had a moral delicacy and a richness of heart that I never saw and never expect to see equaled,' wrote William James.[37] *Richness of heart* fits exquisitely, as you feel when you read Child's letters, with their singular wealth of overflowing, almost caressing tenderness. Love was an essential, perhaps the essential element of felicity, in his universe: 'I wish we could live a thousand years on this pleasant earth, under this bright sky, being happy or growing happier always. . . . Only may we have love where we go.' [38] And if he had tenderness for those beyond his own hearth, we can divine, though we are left mainly to divine, what he felt for those about it. How charming is his relish for the quiet evening at home, when he is free to read to those he loves, Chaucer, or Don Quixote, or Dante, or the old songs which made at once the labor and the relaxation of his life! It is only the fullest allowance for this tenderness that enables us to understand and not misunderstand the warmth of affection in the letters written in later years to a young girl for whom the gentle scholar cherished a peculiar fondness. 'He always had,' wrote Mrs. Child, 'from the beginning of my knowledge of him friendships with women, at first near his own age, with whom he habitually corresponded, and whose letters came like fresh breezes from without.' [39] The play of humor, of melancholy, of imagination, of sympathy, in these letters, is as winning as that of sunshine upon a summer brook.

III

So much for the man's outer life and relations with his fellows. The inner life is equally attractive. Of course reading played a large part in it. Not that Child appears to have been an indiscriminate and omnivorous reader: he was too busy and thorough a worker in his own field. But he read largely in various sorts of books, and, above all, he was passionately fond of poetry and of imaginative writing. The great English poets entered into the very tissue of the life of his spirit. Chaucer, Milton, Spenser were his daily companions, and their rich and varied splendor was so inwoven with his own mode of expression that it is often difficult to distinguish between them. 'When the charm of poetry goes,' he says, 'it seems to me best not to stay. If the world is nothing but Biology and Geology, let's get quickly to some place which is more than that.' [40] As for Shakespeare, the intimate affinity between them is delightful to follow. It was not merely the affection of a scholar and expounder for his theme; it was a close sympathy between two spirits which looked at the world with the same gentle tolerance, the same humorous comprehension, the same infinite love. The Shakespearean turn of phrase, even more than that of the other poets, had become so much Child's own, that one is constantly wondering where Shakespeare ends and where Child begins. 'I see that you are of no age, of Adam's years,' he writes to Lowell,[41] and one feels that the words must be Shakespearean. Or again, 'As she has a sweet, low voice, truth comes mended from her lips.' [42] Especially is there luxuriant delight in the Shakespearean characters, the Shakespearean women. That exquisite idealization of flesh and blood, which Shakespeare managed to embody in his heroines, appealed exactly to Child's temperament, and he is never tired of referring to the charm of Viola and Rosalind, of Miranda and Hermione. 'Those plays,' he cries, 'have enriched the world more than all books taken together.' [43]

In matters of abstract thought one feels something as with general reading, that Child did not make them peculiarly his business. And this was not from the defect of an intelligence, large and acute enough to grapple with any philosophical problem whatsoever, but wholly from love of the concrete, from simple, genial appreciation of what could be warmly touched and felt, instead of an endless groping in barren regions of unremunerative thought. He slipped away from the profounder difficulties, because he felt that the human spirit might be better occupied. 'My thoughts have been deeply tinged with mortality all through. That means that all the questions which we can't answer have been weighing on my mind. But if I can't answer them, I can turn them.' [44] In Madame de Sévigné's pretty phrase, *il faut glisser sur les pensées et ne pas les approfondir*. And for such turning a temperament like Child's found, as did Lamb, the solution of humor exquisitely helpful, not bitter mockery, not cynical irony, but a gentle, whimsical sense of the insignificance of human effort and bustle in the face of the vast problems and difficulties of eternity. 'I should have wreathed my thanks and my delight in some of my customary folly.' [45] Just as such lyrical, gracious, customary folly wreathes the delight and the wonder and the questioning of those airy creatures, the Shake-

spearean clowns, whom this quiet scholar loved
enough perhaps to call them brothers. Touchstone
and Feste also turned the great questions, because
they could not and did not care to answer them.

And as with Lamb, and with the lovely Shakespearean dream-children, the customary folly and
trifling were always close to the sorrow of the world,
its pity and its tears, were merely a relief from them,
a screen from them. This remote, secluded scholar,
especially as life and friends slipped away from
him, felt the agony and strain, felt the dumb effort
at adjustment in a universe of apparent distortion
and incoherent, irrelevant misery. 'My foot used
to feel so firm on the earth; now I should not be
surprised to see the heavens roll up as a scroll and
the hollow crust we walk on vanish into thin air the
next minute.' [46] There are even times when the
depression seems despairing: 'Yesterday I all but
wished that things would cease.' [47]

But amid these shadows the struggling spirit had
always the comfort of profound religious belief, to
which it clung perhaps more ardently because the
basis was emotional rather than intellectual. At
times this emotional element even responded to the
charm of Catholicism, so alluring to souls mysti-
cally and æsthetically disposed: 'When such voices

226

come to me, I feel as if I were all but ready to take
a step. There is a glamor in the recurrence which
for the moment subdues rationalism and reason.
There was a time when perhaps I could not have
resisted the fascination, for it is a fascination, an
enchantment.' [48] And at all times the secure reli-
ance of God, the firm assurance of the future,
offered unfailing comfort in the storms and tempests of this uncertain world.

Sometimes this assurance manifested itself in
shrewd, homely, brief phrases, as in the remark to
Gummere, 'I *could* send a letter of condolence to
James Lowell. For I am one of those old fools *who
think that we go on.*' [49] Again it flowed out in sweet
and solemn amplitude, as in the letter of condolence
itself: 'It has not entered into man's heart to conceive what is preparing, a life to which this is exile;
a delight beyond all that poetry, roses, skies can
give.... And who that is not blinded or deafened
by misery or grief believes that the insubstantial
pageant is to dissolve or fade? What, the man who
wrote those words? Or better, the man that suffered on the cross? Or the sweet pure souls we
have known?' [50] Yet again, it played about the
great problems with gracious tenderness: 'Don't let
the poets falter, or where shall we be? Though I

don't value the philosophers very much, their talk frightens me like ghost stories. When I go back to the poets, I realize I have been fooled.' [51]

And the fine sensibility, the quick and ready response to external suggestion, showed itself in all sides of emotional life. Nature? He was prompt to seize its charm in books, he was even prompter to seize the charm in reality. The delicate, fleeting touches of natural appreciation in the old songs instantly appealed to him. Thus he notes in one example: 'The landscape background of the first two stanzas has often been praised, and its beauty will never pall. It may be called landscape or prelude, for both eyes and ears are addressed.' [52] As for the flowers and the clouds and stars about him, his eyes were ever open to them, and not one of their aspects of grace and radiance was missed. The chill and loneliness of autumn had their attraction: 'I like to go about on fallen leaves and offer the waning world my reverent sympathy. But now there is not a leaf to fall; it would be a bare, gray, chilly northeast day but for the light that comes from you.' [53] And the rapture of spring is welcomed with an accordant ecstasy: 'But when squills and crocuses (not circuses, though I dote on them and they are spring pleasures) and Spring

Beauty come (snow-drops have been trying to open for a fortnight), I expect to cast my slough like other reptiles and to snap my fingers at books.' [54]

For all forms of art there is the same eager appreciation; but undoubtedly the form that appealed to him most was music. He loved it in its subtlest, most ethereal development, the string quartets of Beethoven and Mozart. He loved it in the solemn, impressive masses of the Catholic Church. 'If anything could carry me over, it would be the Masses. They ought to be true; they must be true to something that cannot be lightly estimated.' [55] And in his rapturous catalogue of the enjoyments of this world — simple and complex alike — the music of Beethoven has its conspicuous place: 'Ah, what a world — with roses, sunrise and sunset, Shakespeare, Beethoven, brooks, mountains, birds, maids, ballads — why can't it last, why can't everybody have a good share?' [56]

It will be noted that ballads form the climax of this list of lovely things and with what we have seen of Child's temperament it will be understood that his love for the old songs was far more than the mere scholar's absorption in his erudite specialty. He entered fully into their romantic, riotous atmosphere, as Scott did. He reveled in their color,

229

their naïve, swift, simple tempests of passion and laughter. Their rude music always awoke an answering echo in his spirit. He was condemned to live in the academic, somewhat formal conventions of a New England college town, and he accepted those conventions outwardly with all due observance, no man more so. But inwardly he felt the restraint of them, felt himself cabined, cribbed, confined, rebelled with humorous vigor and indignation. 'I am too much impromptu,' he sighs; 'I ought to live with more prevision and art.' [57] With what mischievous enjoyment he quotes the comment of a French friend upon the Cambridge ladies: '*Bonnes mères de famille probes*, as Mlle. Le Clerc said of the women of Cambridge (she added *mais pas un attrait*).' [58] How whimsically pathetic is his illustration of the conflict between song and work: 'I drop my work any half an hour to go out and see if another adonis is springing or a meadow rue showing its claret-colored head. So false are fables: *la cigale ayant chanté tout l'été*, etc. One should work all winter to be ready to sing all summer, and sing all summer to be able to work the winter through. One or the other one must do, sing or work. I find that I cannot work if I go out under the pretence of just looking at this or that, and I hoped for a rain yesterday (not very earnestly) to keep me indoors.' [59]

Into these staid, decorous surroundings of prosaic propriety the great, loud, sweet old songs swept like a burst of wind and sunshine, and stirred the childish professorial heart to laughter and tears. How winning is Gummere's picture of Child humorously enlarging on the idle, trivial, mirthful matter that enchanted him: '"Preposterous!" he said, "to have to work in such stuff when you could have Young's 'Night Thoughts' or Cowper's 'Task' for the asking. The impudence of the thing!" And he suddenly broke into a kind of chant, reciting the last stanza of the rollicking ballad, and ended in a burst of laughter. He was fairly "going" now, and went on, in a kind of prose parody of that highly moral strain with which Chaucer concludes the "Troilus," to bewail his task of dealing with so many bandits, outlaws, roisterers, silly girls, Lord Lovels, and other chuckle-heads of tradition, setting withal a harmless little trap of quotation, as characteristic as might be. "You remember the line,

'Of Jove, Apollo, of Mars, of swich canaille?'"

he asked, with a sly emphasis on the last word.' [60]

In short, the release from the tameness and monotony of daily life that some of us find in the mystery story, he found more romantically and poetically in the primitive passions and elementary tragedy and comedy of popular song.

IV

And then there were the roses. Child's devotion to them seemed to grow and develop and become richer and more satisfying with the growing years. I do not know that he was a scientific botanist, though one would think that the admiring pupil of Mrs. Ripley might have imbibed something of her enthusiasm in this direction. But he knew and loved roses as if they were intimate friends. With what complacent delight does he reel off long lists of the names of them. With what true collector's eagerness does he indulge himself and deny himself: 'But I have had no time . . . all day till the afternoon, when I took to reading a rose catalogue, which resulted in my ordering more roses, which resulted in remorse, which resulted in my tearing up the order.' [61]

No doubt the cult of roses, like other cults, had its trials and drawbacks. Incessant toil was necessary to attain perfection, toil which distracted from other things, toil which made its importunate demands just when aged limbs were stiffest and weariest; and even with the extreme toil perfection could hardly be attained. There were the insects to combat with forever. 'Saving your presence,' said Child to a young lady, 'I will crush this insect.' And the young lady answered aptly, 'I certainly would not have my presence save him.' [62] While, with all the toil, and after the elimination of all the insects, there was still the eternal tragedy of decay and death. Roses, like fair women, and even sooner, must fade and perish, no matter what delight you found in them, or what pains you took to make them last: 'You write to one from whose lips the cup of bliss has ever been dashed at the moment when he could sip — and a chalice in which floated the fennel's bitter leaf regularly substituted; one born to be illuded and eluded in all things, even as in his simple confidence that roses at least would escape the common lot and be allowed to unfold all the charm which Nature endears them with only to balk them and me.' [63] And again: 'Much of this turbidness comes from seeing the short and perilous life of my roses. I cannot bear to witness the world's dealing with such perfection of beauty and nobleness. It is to-day quite too utterly crushing. I wish I had nothing but dahlias to look at. For the twentieth time I repent me that I ever lived to know what roses are.' [64]

Yet, as with all supreme and overwhelming passions, one returns to roses, in spite of failure and discouragement and decay. 'Such will say of the Rose, as of Love, the grand passion I mean, that all other pleasures are not worth its pains.' [65] What if the beauty fades, has but a brief and transient ecstasy? Shall we not toil for it and enjoy it and adore it all the more on that account? It is such a haunting beauty, such a tantalizing and at the same time satisfying beauty! 'When I was considerably older than you (I was once so young, *et in Arcadia ego!*) I could scarcely sleep for love of plants.' [66] Also, with this passion, as not with some others, we can compound with conscience by sharing the delight with our fellows. We can scatter beauty broadcast, we can give away roses as well as enjoy them. How charming are the stories of the poor children who used to crowd round the gate and be regaled with crimson beneficence. 'Yesterday I gave away eight or nine noble nosegays and supplied some thirty ragamuffin children besides. There was no end to the "Ohs!" My garden was as full as the sky with stars. You ought to have seen them. There is plenty left.' [67]

FRANCIS JAMES CHILD

Music, love, ballads, roses! These surely weave
the tissue of a charming life. 'Superstitions? I
have very few: love of women, roses (including
apple-blossoms), popular poetry, Shakespeare, my
friends, wild flowers, trees, violin music, *voilà!*' [68]
But roses seem to predominate and to incarnadine
the whole with their involving glory. One thinks
of the almost mystical worship of the rose, which
has haunted all the centuries, the ancients, with
their blooms of Paestum and the perpetual recurrence in the Anthology, *baia men alla rhoda, peu de
choses mais roses*, the sensuous hymn of Tasso and
Spenser:

'So passeth, in the passing of a day,
  Of mortall life the leafe, the bud, the flowre;
  Ne more doth florish after first decay,
  That earst was sought to deck both bed and bowre
  Of many a Lady, and many a Paramowre!
  Gather therefore the Rose whilest yet is prime,
  For soone comes age that will her pride deflowre:
  Gather the Rose of love whilest yet is time,
  Whilest loving thou mayst loved be with equall crime,' [69]

the intenser, simple cry of Shakespeare,

'For nothing this wide universe I call,
  Save thou, my rose, in it thou art my all.' [70]

And one feels that Child himself would be not

235

AS GOD MADE THEM

unwilling to have us end with a bit of old song, which he would perhaps forgive for not being of the people because of its roses:

> 'Oh, bury me under the red-rose tree.
> For life was a frolicsome thing to me,
> Without desire, without regret,
> And what I did with it I forget.'

VII
PORTRAIT OF A SCIENTIST
ASA GRAY

CHRONOLOGY

Asa Gray

Born, Oneida County, New York, November 18, 1810.
Graduated Fairfield Medical School, 1830.
Appointed Professor, University of Michigan, 1838.
In Europe, 1838–1839.
Appointed Professor, Harvard, 1842.
Married Jane L. Loring, May 4, 1848.
In Europe, 1850–1851.
In Europe, 1868–1869.
In Europe, 1887.
Died, January 30, 1888.

ASA GRAY

ASA GRAY

I

UNTIL the study of birds began to rival it, the study of flowers was the most popular form of science, and to educated Americans of a generation ago, especially women, Gray's 'Manual' was almost as familiar as the Bible, Shakespeare, or the cook-book. It was said with justice, shortly after Asa Gray's death, 'More than any man who has lived, not excepting Agassiz, he spread and popularized the love and knowledge of natural history in America.' ¹ Yet, though Gray's name is widely familiar, his career was so quiet and so busy with his peculiar occupations that the dignity and beauty of his character are not known to his countrymen as they deserve to be. Moreover, it is not so easy to illustrate his inner life as is the case with some of his distinguished contemporaries. He wrote much, and the two solid volumes of his correspondence might seem to offer an extensive record of what he thought and felt. But he had not the singular gift of revealing himself that belonged, for instance, to his friend Darwin, whose candor and outspokenness are equaled only by his perfect modesty. Gray tells us of his work, of his travels, of the sights he sees, of the people he meets. He tells us little of himself. Yet the task of divining that self from obscure clues and trifling suggestions is all the more fascinating.

Asa Gray was a thorough American. You read it in his face, with its quick, eager, expressive sympathy, its shrewd benignity. The busy, ardent, hasty American temperament was manifest in his movements, and in his clear-cut, decisive speech. He was born in Oneida County, New York, in 1810. He had a vigorous, out-of-door, manual, rather isolated childhood. Like John Brown, he worked at tanning, and always remembered it as 'a lonely and monotonous occupation.'[2] Somewhat later he contrived to get a medical training, which was all the formal academic discipline he ever had. But botany soon took possession of him and botany became the whole of his life. After various wanderings and vicissitudes, he settled down in Cambridge and with his headquarters there worked as hard as any man ever worked at his favorite pursuit, writing and publishing enormously, yet when he died in 1888 leaving his great work on the 'Synoptical Flora of North America' incomplete.

Though his life was given to botany, Gray was

by no means a man of one idea. He had a clear
and active intelligence, which left few subjects un-
probed and unillumined. He did not need the
academic discipline which was denied him; for he
read from childhood, all sorts of things, and with
profit. One day his father sent him to hoe corn,
then went out and found him reading. He was told
he might finish his task and afterwards read comfortably or sit out all day in the hot sun with his
book. He chose the sun and book. 'I made up my
mind he might make something of a scholar,' said
his father, 'but he would never make a farmer.' [3]
And a scholar he was. He read novels, poetry,
travels, sermons, anything. It is interesting to see
how he enlivens and enlightens scientific disserta-
tion with bits from Shakespeare, choosing such
passages as are not hackneyed or part of the
quoter's common stock.

And the vivid precision of his intellect is as
notable as its activity and breadth. He writes with
the careful directness that shows direct thinking.
In fact he was always an admirable writer, had the
ease and facility which are apt to accompany
lucidity. His insistence upon the clear and intelligible handling of a subject is well shown by the
anecdote of the pupil whom he forced to write an

essay six times over before it was accepted. 'I mentally resolved each time,' says the pupil, 'that I would not re-write it; but I did re-write it; and was obliged to continue doing so until he thought it might be allowed to pass. It was the most helpful lesson I ever received in the art of stating things.' 4

Gray constantly applied this clear, unclouded intellectual apparatus to the profounder spiritual interests. He was reticent about his religious feeling, did not exhibit it inappropriately, and his piety had no tinge of gloom or sadness. Life was a cheerful thing to him. So was death: 'I do not call death sad.' 5 But he was quietly firm all his life in an enlightened Christian orthodoxy. Only the orthodoxy was large, charitable, and progressive. Of the doctrines of the Bible he said: 'It cannot be that in all these years we have learned nothing new of their meaning and uses to us, and have nothing still to learn; nor can it be that we are not free to use what we learn in one line of study to limit, correct, or remodel the ideas which we obtain from another.' 6

As he kept his mind open, so he kept his eyes open. In his extensive and repeated journeys all beauty touched him, that of art as well as that of flowers. Melrose is 'the most beautiful ruin I have ever seen or expect to see; more beautiful than I had imagined.' [7] The cathedral of Antwerp delights him, 'the chime at the beginning of the hour still rings in our ears. We have never tired of listening to it' — [8] and the cathedrals of Spain. He discovers Murillo with rapture: 'We now know Murillo and rank him next to Titian, and in feeling and delicacy much above him.' [9]

Nor was he indifferent to the general practical concerns of life. He watched the movements of American democracy with keen interest. Above all, the eagerness and enthusiasm of his nature show in his passionate patriotism throughout the Civil War. His English scientific correspondents were of the class that was inclined to sympathize with the South and he gives them his opinion of his own country and of theirs with a candor that bites and stings. 'It does seem that all England wishes us to be weak and divided,' he writes to Darwin, who was more sympathetic than some others; 'perhaps that is good national policy. But the more that is so, the more necessary it is for us to vindicate our integrity at whatever cost.' [10] With what ardent bitterness does he express his 'hopes of hanging leaders of the rebellion, exiling a good many, and pardoning all the rank and file who will come back with a good grace to their allegiance. If they will not, let them beware.' [11] And it is not words alone. He gladly gives his money and would go into the ranks, if he had youth and strength. 'I pray Congress to put on taxes, five per cent direct on property and income, and heavy indirect besides. What is property! I would fight till every cent is gone, and would offer my own life freely; so I do not value the lives or property of rebels above my own.' [12]

It must not be supposed that this readiness to give money was prompted by any superfluity of means. Gray had no fortune to start with and acquired little as he went on. It is pathetic to see the meagre returns which came from his early teaching and scientific effort. His life-work might bring him reputation and happiness. It certainly did not bring him profit. But he accepted this view at an early stage: 'My moderate wishes would require no very large sum, and I have no great desire to be rich.' [13] He was frugal, thrifty, and self-controlled in everything. Vices did not tempt him and he had no time and no taste for luxuries. As a boy he learned to smoke, that is, he overcame the preliminary distaste. But one evening he said to himself, as he sat with his cigar before the fire:

'Really, I am beginning to like it. It will become a habit; I shall be dependent upon it.' [14] And he threw the cigar away. Such a temperament did not need riches. He had enough for his own wants, enough to give to others, and enough to forward materially the one great interest that appealed to him more than diversion, whether costly or not.

For I do not find that he had much play in his life. Perhaps it would be better to say that he took his work in the spirit of play, so buoyant and eager was he in the pursuit of it. The ordinary sports and amusements, with which most of us vary the dull routine, demanded hours that he could ill spare. There is indeed in his letters one charming picture of domestic recreation. 'My wife is much amused by your backgammon reminiscence,' he writes to Darwin. 'For the year past we have a way of getting on most peacefully. I sit by her side and play solitaire with two packs of cards, she looks on and helps, and when we don't succeed, there is nobody to "flare up" against but luck.' [15] But in general his days were all work and in the evening he wrote botanical textbooks for fun.

Yet the chief end of social amusement, that of increasing human contact and kindliness, was completely attained in Gray's case by the spontaneous warmth of his own nature, which needed no urging to go out and touch other mens' hands and hearts. He was a creature of sympathy and affection, as appears first in his love of animals and zest for their companionship. The story of his dogs is delightful. He would leave even asters to rollick with them. They lived with him so closely that they learned to imitate his diet: 'Not so much, he would say, from any preference for oysters and dry toast, as that they were ambitious to do as far as possible what he did.' [16]

When it came to human beings, Gray was always cordial and cheerful and made people feel at home. He was married somewhat late in life, but the match seems to have been one of tender devotion and affection. There were no children and on this point there is a curious sentence of Gray's, which I do not wholly understand: 'We have no children (which I regret only that I have no son to send to the war).' [17] This suggests the still more striking remark of Darwin, himself a devoted husband and father: 'Children are one's greatest happiness, but often and often a still greater misery. A man of science ought to have none — perhaps not a wife; for then there would be nothing in this wide world worth caring for, and a man might (whether he could is another question) work away like a Trojan.' [18] In any case, Gray was singularly fond of the children of others, liked to talk with them and romp with them and listen to their little joys and sorrows. And he had the same ready sympathy with their elders, did not give the impression that he ought to be doing something else instead of attending to you, as do so many wise and useful persons. What a model picture of a scholar and worker is the following: 'He was preëminently a companionable man, delighting in his friends, very vivacious, and always looking at his experiences with the eyes of fresh youthfulness, as though his whole business was to have a good time.' [19]

This general human kindliness was amplified into a particular affection for those who were near to him in his favorite study. He had many scientific friends, and their tenderness for him is as marked as his for them. His collaboration with Torrey had a striking charm of gracious reciprocity. He cherished an almost lifelong devotion to the Hookers, father and son, and they returned it, Joseph writing publicly, after his friend's death, of 'his bright intelligence, genial disposition, and charming personality.' [20] Professor Goodale's assertion of the regard of those who were constantly working with

Gray at Cambridge is equally impressive: 'To the affection which every member of this Academy [of Arts and Sciences] felt for him was added, in the case of his colleagues, associated in the work of teaching, and brought into daily contact with him, a feeling almost of reverence for a patience which never overstepped its bounds.' [21]

Patience in a teacher goes a long way, and it is remarkable that with so quick and petulant a nature Gray had so much of it. Even the printers, with whom he had extensive dealings, admired him for the forbearance which tempered his shrewdness. 'He never upbraided anybody. A mistake was a mistake in his view, and once corrected, it was lost to his mind, however it might grieve him on its first discovery.' [22] The testimony of his pupils is the same. He himself declares that he could be severe. 'You know I can scold. So I gave him about half a dozen words that made him open his eyes wide; and I do not think that he, nor any of that division, will venture upon anything of the kind again very soon.' [23] But he had little use for severity, because he kept everybody too busy for mischief. He was a worker and made others work. And he could do this because he had the two characteristics that make work easy and profitable. In the first place he was clear, knew what he wanted of himself and of those who were working under him. All agree that the chief merit of his textbooks is clearness, order, system. He never wrote down to young people, never descended to the silliness that disfigures so much of the so-called nature-teaching. But what he said could be understood and applied, at once bred thought and clarified it. And then he was helpful. He could stir a dull student and cheer a bright one in discouragement and difficulty. And he was always ready to give what he had, even money, so far as his moderate means would allow. He carried on a vast correspondence, answered questions concisely but amply, and was so sympathetic and responsive that, as a good judge says, 'it is little wonder that he held all the younger botanists of the country in the hollow of his hand.' [24]

In short, he wanted to commend the love of flowers to his countrymen, and he had a surprising faculty of doing it. How vivid is the picture of one of his western trips when 'the conductor of the train was at last almost in despair at the scattering of his passengers to grab what they could in the short halts, as they became inspired by seeing Dr. Gray rush as the engine slowed, to catch all within reach.' [25] To catch all that was within reach and make it yield all its secrets and tell those secrets to others — that was the overmastering aim of this eager heart, whose essence is well gathered up in the verses of Lowell, written for Gray's seventieth anniversary:

'Just Fate, prolong his life well spent,
    Whose indefatigable hours
Have been as gaily innocent
    And fragrant as his flowers.' [26]

II

The charm of these human relations of Gray's shows the ideal influence of the scientific spirit. The study of facts in and for themselves, with its constant suggestion of the insignificance of man, the long days and years of patient observation, above all the unwearied attempt to understand all men and all things, should foster tolerance, gentleness, patience, sympathy. No doubt great scientists have been irritable and ill to consort with. But the highest, finest type must reflect something of the immortal impersonality of the thoughts with which they live. It is his admirable embodiment of this ideal that makes Darwin the man as interesting as any of his theories. And if Gray did not quite attain the perfection of Darwin, he had very much about him of Darwin's human attractiveness.

As the scientific spirit should make men friendly and kindly-disposed to their fellows in general, so it should produce the same result infinitely more in regard to those who are engaged in similar pursuits. Not rivalry, not self-seeking, not the desire to force or forward one's own schemes or theories should prevail, but always the willingness to recognize other points of view, to see the other side. In the admirable words of Darwin, 'As I am writing my book, I try to take as much pains as possible to give the strongest cases opposed to me.' [27] Here again it must be admitted that the history of Science affords lamentable instances of defection from the ideal. There has always been and will always be far too much of self-advertising, pedantry, dogmatism, and profitless controversy. But these things come from the noisy, the bustling, from those who are more interested in themselves than in their cause. The thousands of patient, devoted workers, who toil quietly, are not heard of, but their labor tells.

Such in his essential spirit and in the ardor of his assiduous effort was Asa Gray, though his extensive popularization of his favorite study and his ready pen gave him more prominence than falls to some who are equally industrious. When he had drawn his conclusions carefully, he did not hesitate to affirm them. But none knew better than he the difficulty of drawing such conclusions and the constant probability that you may be wrong and others right: 'Judgments formed to-day — perhaps with full confidence, perhaps with misgiving — may to-morrow, with the discovery of new materials or the detection of some before unobserved point of structure, have to be weighed and decided anew.' [28] How charming is his recognition of Darwin's extraordinary gift of insight and his deference to it: 'What a skill and genius you have for these researches! Even for the structure of the flower of the Ophyrideæ I have to-night learned more than I ever knew before.' [29] How equally charming is his modest reply when offered the privilege of lecturing at the Lowell Institute: 'Mr. Lowell offered at once to engage me for two or three years; but I told him he had best wait to see how I succeeded.' [30]

It is true that Gray had a logical mind and an eager spirit. When a subject interested him, when he had espoused a cause, he was ready to discuss, to debate, even to argue with much vehemence. Here is a pretty picture of such a friendly controversy, drawn by one who knew him well: 'Both were excited, and the doctor showed his excitement in his characteristically self-forgetful way, by moving or jumping nervously about the room, sitting on the floor, lying down flat, but laughing and sending sparks out of his eyes, and plying his arguments and making his witty thrusts all the while.' [31] Gray himself indicates the same tendency, with more concise self-reproach: 'Most uncivilly, I fear, I fell almost into a wrangle with him directly. He even seemed to think us on the whole a bigoted set here in Cambridge — rather a novel view to us.' [32] The most marked display of this argumentative disposition was in the controversy with Agassiz over the theories of Darwin, a controversy which for the time produced a good deal of feeling and even partisanship in Cambridge academic circles. [33] The contest took the form of public debates in 1859, and by the admission of his own biographer Agassiz had rather the worst of it, though the biographer attributes this to his lack of skill as a debater and to the somewhat discourteous tactics of his adversary. [34] The strained state of local feeling at this time is humorously suggested in the little comment of the geologist Lesley: 'While Agassiz was talking to me about the senselessness of scientific quarrels, Gray came and sat down beside me.' [35]

But in these little professional alarums and incursions there was not an atom of personal bitterness or malevolence. 'He was a clear and close reasoner himself,' says Mrs. Gray, 'and thus impatient of defective reasoning or a confused statement in others. He was quick, too, in turning his opponents' weapons against them.' [36] But underneath it all his one desire was to get at the light, to brush away prejudice and old convention and insincere habits of thought: 'Taking it for granted that you rather like to be criticized, as I am sure I do, when the object is the surer establishment of truth.' [37] And no discussion or argument invalidated his fundamental soul of amiability and kindliness. There was not a trace of grudge or envy in any of his controversies. And all his allusions to Agassiz show the same cordial and enduring regard which appears in the affectionate tribute written after his death.

More than this, Gray was always ready to help and encourage all who were working faithfully for the cause he loved. This shows most in the immense extent of his labors as a critic and reviewer. For fifty years he discussed in print the chief contributions to the science of botany, and the two solid volumes of his collected scientific papers contain but a very small part of his production. All this mass of critical work is said by those competent to judge to be thoughtful, careful, profitable, and suggestive. Gray had an extraordinary faculty of going to the essential secret of a book, plucking it out, and conveying it in a form that would be at once interesting and instructive to his readers. His reviews are much more than learned, they are readable and entertaining. How playfully attractive is the grace with which he introduces his own book, when discussing that of another: 'A work which is for that district what Gray's "Manual" is for the northern section of our common country. Having said this, modesty prevents more particular eulogium. If experience annually shows that the work with which this volume is compared is not yet perfect, but still requires many minor emendations, notwithstanding long pains-taking and repeated revisions, it may be expected that equal experience will reveal similar imperfections in the new and untried work.' [38]

In all this critical effort Gray's aim was constructive, to sustain and advance, not to blight or discourage. He could be outspoken, could deprecate what was futile and condemn what was worthless. To one who protested against such severity he wrote these just and admirable words: 'In my heart

I would have been more tender than you, but I cannot afford to be. I am, from my present position before the world, a critic, and I cannot shrink from the duty which such a position imposes upon me. If you were in the position that I am, with a short life and a long task before you, and just as you thought the way was clear for progress, some one should dump cart-loads of rubbish in your path, and you had to take off your coat, roll up your sleeves, and spend weeks in digging that rubbish away before you could proceed, I should not suppose you would be a model of amiability.' [39] But in the main the rubbish is disregarded or gently thrust aside and the critic dwells upon what is worth reading, worth knowing. As Professor Goodale excellently expressed it: 'He could find faults, but not as a fault-finder: his aim was always to secure improvement.' [40]

III

But these human relations were, after all, secondary, subordinate to the pure scientific instinct of learning, of knowing, of advancing daily a little further in the vast field of possible research; and the study of Gray's life shows everywhere the satisfaction of recognizing this instinct, of yielding to it, of following wherever it might lead.

ASA GRAY

It is curious to consider how far ambition, the desire for praise and approval, enters into such a life-pursuit as this. As Gray progressed in his career, he received honors, testimonials, flattering commendations. How much did they mean to him? He made textbooks. Did he feel, as one of his colleagues used to say playfully, that the greatest pleasure in life would be to see the girls riding in the cars to school carrying Lane's Latin Grammar under their arms? Gray had a just and manly sense of the value of his work. Has not every man whose work is really worth doing? He could say with perfect frankness of one of his own lectures: 'It would be mere affectation for me to pretend not to know — as I well do — that it is one of the best scientific lectures that have ever been delivered in Boston.' [41] The glimpses of direct ambition that peep out in his correspondence are singularly attractive. 'It will probably tend to advance my interests, as I certainly wish it may, the object of my ambition being high and honorable, as well as moderate.' [42] He fondles and caresses glory as a child does a toy, whether it comes in the shape of a mountain-peak, called after him, or a pigweed: 'Hooker has a curious new genus of Chenopodiaceæ, from the Rocky Mountains, figured for the

"Icones," which he wishes to call Grayia! I am quite content with a Pigweed; and this is a very queer one.'[43] But it is evident that such notoriety is a surface matter, quite distinct from the serious business of life, and the fundamental spirit in which he worked is admirably indicated in the noble words of his own eulogy of Joseph Henry: 'He never courted publicity; not from fastidious dislike, still less from contempt of well-earned popular applause, but simply because he never thought of it.'[44]

For Gray's life was as busy, as fruitfully busy, as any man's ever was. He had in the main excellent health and husbanded it wisely for large accomplishment. He had immense, unbounded energy, energy which not only did not flag but leaped to new tasks as if it enjoyed them and only asked for more. When he was in the field, he seemed inexhaustible. Even in later life he could outwalk men of half his years. Vigor, achievement, seemed written on his nervous frame and restless motions. 'Dr. Gray was noticeable throughout his life for his alertness. In the street he was usually on a half run, for he never allowed himself quite time enough to reach his destination leisurely. . . . As his motions were quick, so that he seemed always ready for a spring, so he found instant relaxation by throwing himself on the floor when tired, to rest, like a child.'[45]

He not only worked quickly, he worked easily. That is, his work had the appearance of ease, because he knew how to direct his effort, to go right to the central point of any difficulty, without floundering, without blundering. He had a wonderful memory, not only for plants but for everything else, could retain what was useful to him and reproduce it at will. 'To see Gray run through a bundle of newly arrived plants was a revelation to the cautious plodder. Every character he had ever met seemed vivid in his memory and ready to be applied instantly; and the bundle was 'sorted' with a speed that defied imitation. It seemed like intuition, but it was vast experience backed by a wonderful memory; perhaps it could be called genius.'[46]

Yet in the ease and speed there was no neglect of thoroughness. Unfaltering perseverance is the first evident requisite for doing the sort of work that Gray did and doing it well, and no man ever cultivated perseverance more assiduously. He hated to alter his arrangements even for better: 'I have such a dislike to the appearance of vacillation which results from changing one's plans when fully formed.' ⁴⁷ He was bound to succeed and along the line which had been laid out after careful deliberation: 'If I don't altogether succeed, neither satisfying myself nor others, I shall not be discouraged, but try again, as I am determined to succeed in the long run.' ⁴⁸ No matter what the pressure might be, the most minute detail must be attended to and attended to properly: 'There is much to be done, and so little time that I often wish I could divide myself into a dozen men, and thus get on faster. Let us, however, take particular pains to do everything thoroughly as far as we go.' ⁴⁹ Most winning of all is the patient devotion to common, ugly things, which many might think beneath their dignity: 'I have been addling my brain and straining my eyes over a set of ignoble Pond-weeds . . . and wasting about as much brain as your dear paternal would expend in an intricate law case, for all of which I suppose nobody will thank me and I shall get no fee. Indeed, few would see the least sense in devoting so much time to a set of vile little weeds. But I could not slight them. The Creator seems to have bestowed as much pains on them, if we may use such a word, as upon more conspicuous things, so I do not see why I should not try to study them out.' ⁵⁰

In all this long career of kindly, beneficent labor there seem to have been few serious drawbacks, difficulties, or discouragements. 'His life has been one of extraordinary tranquillity and enjoyment,' says Norton.[51] But this impression was partly owing to the man's sunny and buoyant temper. 'He was exceedingly hopeful,' says Mrs. Gray, 'and always carried with him a happy assurance that everything was going on well in his absence.'[52] And he himself expresses the same thing, with a charming illustration from his own beloved flowers: 'I have no penchant for melancholy, sober as I sometimes look, but turn always, like the leaves, my face to the sun.'[53] Again, he said, 'I never wanted anything but, when I was ready for it, it came to me.'[54]

Yet all was not perfect success and triumph. In one critical situation he confesses: 'I should despond greatly if I were not of a cheerful temperament.'[55] Throughout his early years there were money difficulties. At least devotion to his favorite pursuit demanded sacrifices that to some would have seemed intolerable. 'Having no income for the last two years, I have been greatly embarrassed, and have struggled through great difficulties, I scarcely know how.'[56] To feel that after such prolonged and strenuous effort his chief work must in

AS GOD MADE THEM

all probability be left unfinished would have been a
cause of bitter complaint to some men. And then
there were the asters. It is the little frets that
break men down, not the great calamities. And
even Gray's serenity almost yielded to the asters.
In his middle years he was toiling at them: 'I have
diligently labored about four months at Asters, in
which, as I have after all not satisfied myself, I can
scarcely hope to satisfy others.' [57] And they tor-
mented him in age, as he himself indicates with
graceful gayety: 'My wife now excuses me to her
friends for outbreaks of ill-humor, the excuse being
that I am at present "in the valley of the shadow
of the Asters." This is *sic itur ad astra*, with a
vengeance.' [58]

Yet these little difficulties and drawbacks did
not count a moment beside the infinitely varied
seduction and fascination of nature. It has been
proved over and over again that few things are so
absorbing as the study of the fleeting forms and
delicate differences that life offers in all its subtle
growth and change. Mere seeing is an exquisite art
and one of immense difficulty, as most of us who
walk through the world with our eyes veiled by
convention and prejudice hardly realize. When
Gautier said, 'I am a man for whom the visible

world exists,' he implied, and justly, that such men
are far from common. Indeed, the universal vision
that Gautier meant is so rare and so hard to attain
that the most skilled observer in science usually con-
fines himself to seeing in one special field and is as
oblivious to others as the ordinary mortal. However this may be, it is certain that the trained observer, like Gray, instantly seizes delicate distinc-
tions and minute details that are quite lost to the
common eye, and finds an inexhaustible interest in
so doing. The mere grasp of fact, pure and simple,
becomes an exquisite employment of the mental
powers. 'To see the plant vividly, to seize the essential features, and then to describe them aptly
was to him as much a matter of individual style as
the production of a literary composition.' [59] Facts,
thus treated in their objective value, grow to be a
theme for reverence. The study and accumulation
of them offers a far more than sufficient purpose for
a lifetime. And any tendency to tamper with them
for speculative ends is little less than a crime. 'For
my part, in respect to the bearings of the distribution of plants, etc., I am determined to know no
theory, but to see what the facts tend to show,
when fairly treated.' [60]

In this way, Gray's own chief importance is

generally recognized to be as a student of facts, as a
systematic botanist, a describer and classifier. He
did not aim primarily to be an original producer of
theories or hypotheses. And he believed that all
such should be received with the utmost caution,
should be tried and tested at every step by close
comparison with the established facts. 'For the
reason that I like the general doctrine, and wish to
see it established, so much the more I am bound to
try all the steps of the reasoning, and all the facts it
rests on impartially, and even to suggest all the adverse criticism I can think of.' [61] Yet he fully appreciated the value of speculation in scientific progress and above all, he had, or always aimed to
have, that first element of the scientific spirit, candor, independence, the entire willingness to follow
truth wherever it leads, no matter what idols are
blasted in the process. For the attitude of mind
which asks common agreement to exclude all disagreeable conclusions he had nothing but contempt:
'He is one of those people who think that if you
shut your eyes hard, it will answer every purpose,'
he says of one who adopted such an attitude. [62] And
I know few finer expressions of philosophical candor
than his remark as to the doctrines which were beginning to prevail about him: 'I have no particular

predilection for any of them; and I have no particular dread of any of the consequences which legitimately flow from them, beyond the general awe and sense of total insufficiency with which a mortal man contemplates the mysteries which shut him in on every side.' [63]

These words were written in regard to the Darwinian theories of Evolution, and the most interesting example of Gray's candor is his acceptance of those theories side by side with his inherited tradition of strict orthodoxy. The drift of his previous studies had quite prepared him to welcome the views of Darwin and he did so with ardor. His ready pen and remarkable power of presenting arguments clearly and concisely made him at once one of Darwin's ablest assistants and exponents in this country. At the same time he never felt that the foundations of his orthodox theology were in the least affected and with perfect sincerity he endeavored to show that nothing in Darwin's hypotheses, as held by Darwin himself, in any way conflicted with the tenets of that theology. The subtlety and ingenuity with which he maintained this position are exceedingly interesting. He reasoned like a lawyer and expatiated like a journalist. It seems as if his naturally logical and ratiocinative

disposition basked in the opportunity of making
up for confinement to fact in the narrower botanical
field by soaring out into a region where speculation
seems always permissible, if rarely conclusive.

It will at once be seen how valuable this assistance was to Darwin. The greatest drawback to his
theories was their supposed tendency to atheism.
And here was an approved scientist, whose orthodoxy could not be questioned, showing that Darwinian Evolution was perfectly compatible with a
devout belief in the Deity of the New and even the
Deity of the Old Testament. Darwin was pro-
portionately grateful. He found in Gray, considered
merely as a scientist, one of his most intelligent
disciples, 'about the most competent judge in the
world,' [64] he calls him, and again, 'you and three
others I put down in my own mind as the judges
whose opinions I should value most of all.' [65] He
writes to Gray: 'You know my book as well as I do
myself; and bring to the question new lines of illustration and argument in a manner which excites
my astonishment and almost my envy.' [66] And he
writes to Jeffries Wyman: 'No one other person
understands me so thoroughly as Asa Gray. If ever
I doubt what I mean myself, I think I shall ask
him.' [67] When to this general comprehension was

added the mighty support against religious narrowness and obloquy, it will easily be understood that Darwin was delighted and could add in the letter just quoted: 'His generosity in getting my views a fair hearing, and not caring himself for unpopularity has been most unselfish — I would say noble.' [68] What would Gray have thought if he had lived to see the theories of Darwin become a vast source of human misery and Darwin himself, so gentle, so humane, get to be regarded as a spectre of evil such as some persons see in Rousseau? But Gray, in his unfailing cheerful optimism, would probably have said that the fault was not that of Darwin but of the pseudo-Darwinians, and that the overruling Providence which guides all things together for good would bring truth out of error in the end.

IV

While these questions and discussions of general theory may form the most exciting part of a scientist's life, they are not the most attractive or the most satisfying. What really counts is the growth of knowledge from day to day, the endless fascination of watching, detecting, recording, of losing your petty existence in the vast, ceaseless, inexplicable expansion of the natural world. This

pleasure is so much taken for granted in the long
career of Gray that we are rather left to divine it
than to read it openly in any specific words of
ecstasy. It is rare that we find anything like Darwin's passionate sentence: 'The delight of sitting on
a decaying trunk amidst the quiet gloom of the
forest is unspeakable and never to be forgotten.' [69]
Yet if we search carefully, there are gleams of the
same passion to be discovered in Gray's letters, as
when he writes in youth of a botanical treatise, 'I
have nearly finished De Candolle's "Théorie Elémentaire." I have devoured it like a novel.' [70] And
the same appears later, in a form concise but intense, when the rediscovery of *Shortia galacifolia*
is announced to him. ' "If you think you have
Shortia, send it on." It was sent. Then came
from Dr. Gray the characteristic postal: "It is so.
Now let me sing my *nunc dimittis*." ' [71] To which he
adds later, 'I did not say, before, that this discovery
has given me a hundred times the satisfaction that
the election into the Institute did.' [72]

Note that this fascinated surrender to the scientific study of the natural world is an altogether
different thing from the æsthetic or the philosophical enjoyment of it. The imagination of Keats
weaves a web of associated beauty about the ex-

ternal detail of the material universe, clothes —
and obscures — it in a tissue of splendor; the speculative instinct of Emerson informs it with subtle
divinity. But the naturalist is satisfied with the limitless, the inexhaustible, the emancipating exercise
of pure intelligence. To know, to know, and ever-
more to know, is enough. There is a suggestive
sentence, which was a favorite with Sainte-Beuve
and is said to be derived from Virgil, one would at
least like to think it his: *On se lasse de tout sauf de
comprendre*, one wearies of everything except to
understand. The phrase is perhaps less applicable
to Gray than to some others, because apparently he
wearied of nothing. But at least he too felt, and
through his writings made thousands of others feel,
how intense and unfailing is the interest of probing
a little, little, little farther into the mystery of
life, of lifting one even insignificant corner of Nature's sweet, vast garment of secrecy, of asserting
the most stimulating, if not the highest of human
powers, the power to understand. Whether one
studies the soul of plants, or the soul of animals, or
the soul of men, *on se lasse de tout sauf de comprendre*.

THE END

NOTES

NOTES

THE titles of books most frequently cited are prefixed to each chapter, with abbreviations used.

I. DANIEL WEBSTER

Curtis, George Ticknor, *The Life of Daniel Webster*, two volumes.
Curtis.
Webster, Daniel, *The Works of* (1853), six volumes. *Works.*
Webster, Daniel, *The Writings and Speeches of*, eighteen volumes, 1903. *Writings.*
Webster, Daniel, *The Private Correspondence of*, two volumes.
Correspondence.
Webster, Daniel, *The Letters of*, edited by C. H. Van Tyne.
Van Tyne.

1. Curtis, vol. II, p. 139.
2. Lecture on 'The Dead of the Cabinet,' by President Tyler, in *The Letters and Times of the Tylers*, by Lyon G. Tyler, vol. II, p. 205.
3. *Memoirs of John Quincy Adams*, September 17, 1841, vol. XI, p. 20.
4. To Fletcher Webster, January 15, 1836, *Correspondence*, vol. II, p. 16.
5. Emerson, 'The Fugitive Slave Law,' in *Miscellanies* (1884), p. 211.
6. Burke, *Works* (Bohn edition), vol. I, p. 407.
7. To Merrill, January 4, 1803, *Correspondence*, vol. I, p. 129.
8. Quoted from Felton, in Curtis, vol. II, p. 669.
9. *The Diary of Philip Hone* (edition 1889), November 29, 1837, vol. I, p. 281.
10. *The Journals of Ralph Waldo Emerson*, February 7, 1843, vol. VI, p. 345.
11. *Life, Letters, and Journals of George Ticknor*, vol. I, p. 330.
12. *Works*, vol. II, p. 134.

NOTES

13. *Life and Letters of Robert Edward Lee*, by J. William Jones, D.D., p. 121.
14. To Mason, April 19, 1829, *Correspondence*, vol. I, p. 477.
15. Curtis, vol. II, p. 215.
16. To Fletcher Webster, July 29, 1846, Van Tyne, p. 339.
17. Calhoun to Clemson, April 3, 1842, *Correspondence* (American Historical Association), p. 508.
18. Plumer, Reminiscences, in *Writings*, vol. XVII, p. 560.
19. Curtis, vol. II, p. 698.
20. *Works*, vol. I, p. 39.
21. *Works*, vol. II, p. 214.
22. Quoted in Norman Hapgood, *Daniel Webster*, p. 61.

II. HENRY CLAY

Clay, Henry, *Life and Speeches* (1854), two volumes. *Speeches.*
Clay, Henry, *Works* (1897), seven volumes. *Works.*
Clay, Henry, *The Private Correspondence of.* *Correspondence.*
Clay, Thomas Hart, *Henry Clay.* Clay.
Colton, Calvin, *Life and Times of Henry Clay.* Colton.
Prentice, George D., *Biography of Henry Clay.* Prentice.
Rogers, Joseph M., *The True Henry Clay.* Rogers.
Schurz, Carl, *Life of Henry Clay*, two volumes. Schurz.

1. J. O. Harrison, *Reminiscences*, in *Century Magazine*, December, 1886, vol. XI, p. 181.
2. Rogers, p. 164.
3. Clay, p. 231.
4. November 19, 1835, *Correspondence*, p. 401.
5. Mrs. Smith to J. B. Smith, March 12, 1829, in *The First Forty Years of Washington Society*, by Mrs. S. H. Smith, p. 301.
6. Mrs. Smith to Mrs. Boyd, December 25, 1835, in *ibid.*, p. 375.
7. Calvin Colton, *The Last Seven Years of the Life of Henry Clay*, p. 56.
8. Colton, vol. I, p. 34.
9. C. W. Coleman, Jr., in *Century Magazine*, December, 1886, vol. XI, p. 167.

NOTES

10. To T. M. Prentiss, February 15, 1807, *Correspondence*, p. 15.
11. Rogers, p. 151.
12. Peter Harvey, *Reminiscences and Anecdotes of Daniel Webster*, p. 218.
13. Story to Todd, March 14, 1823, in *Life and Letters of Joseph Story*, by William W. Story, vol. I, p. 423.
14. Calvin Colton, *The Last Seven Years of the Life of Henry Clay*, p. 52.
15. Rogers, p. 369.
16. Charles Lanman, *The Private Life of Daniel Webster*, p. 130.
17. Ticknor to Prescott, January 16, 1825, in *Life, Letters, and Journals of George Ticknor*, vol. I, p. 350.
18. Harriet Martineau, *Retrospect of Western Travel*, vol. I, p. 242.
19. J. W. Watson, in *North American Review*, November, 1888, vol. 147, p. 589.
20. Rogers, p. 302.
21. M. McDowell, in *Century Magazine*, September, 1895, vol. XXVIII, p. 767.
22. Rogers, p. 31.
23. Rogers, p. 102.
24. *Memoirs of John Quincy Adams*, September 8, 1814, vol. III, p. 32.
25. Colton, vol. I, p. 47.
26. Rogers, p. 163.
27. Oliver Dyer, *Great Senators of the United States Forty Years Ago*, p. 240.
28. Address to Constituents, *Works*, vol. V, p. 303.
29. Thomas H. Benton, *Thirty Years' View*, vol. I, p. 77.
30. Rogers, p. 288.
31. Schurz, vol. II, p. 270.
32. James Ford Rhodes, *A History of the United States from the Compromise of 1850*, vol. I, p. 120.
33. Mrs. Smith to J. B. Smith, March 12, 1829, in *The First Forty Years of Washington Society*, p. 303.
34. J. O. Harrison, in *Century Magazine*, December, 1886, vol. XI, p. 179.
35. *The Writings of Abraham Lincoln*, vol. II, p. 162.

NOTES

36. Rogers, p. 285.
37. Abraham Lincoln, *Writings*, vol. II, p. 165.
38. Rogers, p. 167.
39. Rogers, p. 251.
40. To Brooke, February 18, 1825, *Correspondence*, p. 116.
41. Prentice, p. 245.
42. *Speeches*, vol. II, p. 646.
43. Clay to Committee in New York, August 6, 1837, *Correspondence*, p. 417.
44. Gallatin to James Gallatin, January 29, 1827, in Henry Adams, *The Life of Albert Gallatin*, p. 623.
45. Henry A. Wise, *Seven Decades of the Union*, p. 171.
46. *Memoirs of John Quincy Adams*, December 24, 1817, vol. IV, p. 31.
47. Speech of April 8, 1850, *Works*, vol. VI, p. 412.
48. Speech at Lexington, May, 1829, in Prentice, p. 261.
49. Speech on the Line of the Perdido, December 25, 1810, *Speeches*, vol. I, p. 4.
50. M. McDowell, in *Century Magazine*, September, 1895, vol. XXVIII, p. 767.
51. Abraham Lincoln, *Writings*, vol. II, p. 163.
52. To S. F. Miller, July 1, 1844, *Correspondence*, p. 491.

III. JOHN CALDWELL CALHOUN

Calhoun, John Caldwell Calhoun, *Works*, six volumes.   *Works.*
Calhoun, John C. Calhoun, *Correspondence*, edited by J. Franklin Jameson, in *Fourth Annual Report* of the Historical Manuscripts Commission of the American Historical Association, 1900.   *Correspondence.*
Calhoun, John C., *Life*, 1843 (*Autobiography?*)   *Autobiography.*
Hunt, Gaillard, *John C. Calhoun.*   Hunt.
Meigs, William M., *The Life of John Caldwell Calhoun*, two volumes.   Meigs.

1. Harriet Martineau, *Retrospect of Western Travel*, vol. I, p. 243.
2. Varina Howell Davis, *Jefferson Davis*, vol. I, p. 210.

276

NOTES

3. Meigs, vol. II, p. 110.
4. Varina Howell Davis, *Jefferson Davis*, vol. I, p. 210.
5. Speech on Joint Occupancy, March 16, 1846, *Works*, vol. IV, p. 268.
6. Dr. H. von Holst, *John C. Calhoun*, p. 199.
7. Sarah Mytton Maury, *The Statesmen of America in 1846*, p. 355.
8. Speech on Re-Chartering of Bank, March 21, 1834, *Works*, vol. II, p. 356.
9. Speech on Loan Bill, July 19, 1841, *Works*, vol. IV, p. 11.
10. Speech on Abolition Petitions, February 6, 1837, *Works*, vol. II, p. 631.
11. Edward Channing, *History of the United States*, vol. V, p. 279.
12. To Green, February 10, 1844, *Correspondence*, p. 569.
13. Meigs, vol. II, p. 98.
14. In Sarah Mytton Maury, *The Statesmen of America in 1846*, p. 377.
15. To Abbott Lawrence, May 13, 1845, *Correspondence*, p. 655.
16. To J. E. Calhoun, September 27, 1821, *Correspondence*, p. 197.
17. Charles A. and Mary R. Beard, *The Rise of American Civilization*, vol. I, p. 668.
18. Quoted in Meigs, vol. II, p. 89.
19. To Brown, November 14, 1844, *Correspondence*, p. 628.
20. Sarah Mytton Maury, *The Statesmen of America in 1846*, p. 371.
21. *Autobiography*, p. 69.
22. Miss M. Bates, in *International Magazine*, August-December, 1851, vol. IV, p. 174.
23. To Mrs. Clemson, March 7, 1848, *Correspondence*, p. 745.
24. Mary Boykin Chesnut, *A Diary from Dixie*, March 11, 1861, p. 17.
25. Leopardi, *Pensieri*, XXVII.
26. Meigs, vol. I, p. 166, from Curtis's *Webster*, vol. I, p. 143.
27. To Hammon, February 18, 1837, *Correspondence*, p. 368.
28. Letter of Mrs. Tyler, November 27, 1844, in *The Letters and Times of the Tylers*, by Lyon G. Tyler, vol. II, p. 356.
29. Meigs, vol. II, p. 100, from Foote's *Casket of Reminiscences*, p. 78.
30. Meigs, vol. II, p. 103, from Pinckney, in *Lippincott's Magazine*, vol. LXII, p. 85.

NOTES

31. To Mrs. Floride Calhoun, June 12, 1810, *Correspondence*, p. 115.
32. *Correspondence*, p. 119.
33. To Mrs. Floride Calhoun, September 13, 1810, *Correspondence*, p. 120.
34. To Mrs. Floride Calhoun, June 12, 1810, *Correspondence*, p. 115.
35. Sarah Mytton Maury, *The Statesmen of America in 1846*, p. 376.
36. To Mrs. Floride Calhoun, April 9, 1815, *Correspondence*, p. 128.
37. Crallé MS. quoted in Hunt, p. 314.
38. Sarah Mytton Maury, *The Statesmen of America in 1846*, p. 363.
39. To J. E. Calhoun and A. Burt, August and September, 1831, *Correspondence*, pp. 301, 302.
40. Webster, *Works* (1853), vol. v, p. 369.
41. To Green, March 24, 1847, *Correspondence*, p. 722.
42. To Mrs. Floride Calhoun, December 21, 1811, *Correspondence*, p. 124.
43. To Mrs. Floride Calhoun, September 11, 1806, *Correspondence*, p. 107.
44. Clay to Brooke, December 5, 1824, *The Private Correspondence of Henry Clay*, p. 107.
45. Varina Howell Davis, *Jefferson Davis*, vol. i, p. 210.
46. Oliver Dyer, *Great Senators of the United States*, p. 187.
47. Prioleau, in Meigs, vol. ii, p. 98.
48. Oliver Dyer, *Great Senators*, p. 185.
49. To Van Devanter, August 5, 1831, *Correspondence*, p. 297.
50. To Green, July 27, 1837, *Correspondence*, p. 376.
51. To Garnett, July 3, 1824, *Correspondence*, p. 219.
52. Quoted in Beveridge's *John Marshall*, vol. i, p. 419.

IV. HORACE GREELEY

Greeley, Horace, *Recollections of a Busy Life*.   *Recollections*.
Linn, William Alexander, *Horace Greeley*.   Linn.
Parton, James, *The Life of Horace Greeley*.   Parton.

1. Parton, p. 44.
2. *Recollections*, p. 41.
3. Parton, p. 65.

NOTES

4. *Recollections*, p. 325.
5. *Recollections*, p. 116.
6. From New York *Tribune*, in Parton, p. 276.
7. Parton, p. 429.
8. *Recollections*, p. 104.
9. *Ibid.*
10. *Recollections*, p. 297.
11. Maunsell B. Field, *Memories of Many Men*, p. 317.
12. *Recollections*, p. 335.
13. Greeley to Colonel Tappan, quoted by Rhodes, *History of the United States*, vol. VI, p. 440.
14. Parton, p. 51.
15. Parton, p. 62.
16. Linn, p. 18.
17. *Recollections*, p. 99.
18. Parton, p. 428.
19. *Recollections*, p. 206.
20. Parton, p. 197.
21. *Recollections*, p. 203.
22. *Recollections*, p. 42.
23. *Recollections*, p. 469.
24. *Recollections*, p. 473.
25. *Recollections*, p. 513.
26. Horace Greeley, *What I Know of Farming*, p. vii.
27. *Recollections*, pp. 70, 71, 72.
28. Parton, p. 431.
29. Andrew Dickson White, *Autobiography*, vol. II, p. 538.
30. Linn, p. 66.
31. *Recollections*, p. 195.
32. Linn, p. 108, from Chauncy Depew.
33. *Memoirs of Margaret Fuller Ossoli*, by R. W. Emerson, W. H. Channing, and J. F. Clarke, vol. II, p. 151.
34. Eli Thayer, *A History of the Kansas Crusade*, p. 43.
35. *Recollections*, p. 285.
36. Andrew Dickson White, *Autobiography*, vol. I, p. 160.
37. *Recollections*, p. 508.
38. Horace Greeley, *Hints towards Reform*, p. 45.

NOTES

39. John G. Nicolay and John Hay, *Abraham Lincoln, A History*, vol. II, p. 140.
40. Parton, p. 44.
41. Frederic Bancroft, *Life of William H. Seward*, vol. I, p. 374, from Seward MS., November 24, 1854.
42. Colonel Tappan, quoted in Rhodes, *History of the United States*, vol. VI, p. 440.
43. *Recollections*, p. 322.
44. To friend, in Linn, p. 39.
45. New York *Tribune*, in L. U Reavis, *A Representative Life of Horace Greeley*, p. 495.
46. Edwin Lawrence Godkin, *Life and Letters*, vol. I, p. 167.
47. Godkin to Norton, Godkin, *Life and Letters*, vol. I, p. 292.
48. See Albert Bigelow Paine, *Thomas Nast*, p. 162.
49. From *New Yorker*, in Linn, p. 34.
50. Parton, p. 360.
51. *Recollections*, p. 457.
52. Edwin Lawrence Godkin, *Life and Letters*, vol. I, p. 255.
53. *Recollections*, p. 143.

V. EDWIN BOOTH

Grossmann, Edwina Booth, *Edwin Booth*.   Grossmann.
Winter, William, *Life and Art of Edwin Booth*, revised edition.
                                                Winter, *Life*.
Winter, William, *Other Days*.   *Other Days*.
Winter, *Vagrant Memories*.   *Vagrant Memories*.

1. Royle, article in *Harper's Magazine*, May, 1916, vol. CXXXII, p. 840.
2. Russell Sullivan, *Diary*, June 7, 1893, p. 99.
3. *Other Days*, p. 227.
4. To David G. Anderson, June 20, 1882, Grossmann, p. 232.
5. *Actors and Actresses of Great Britain and the United States*, p. 96.
6. William Webster Ellsworth, *A Golden Age of Authors*, p. 17.
7. Royle, in *Harper's Magazine*, May, 1916, vol. CXXXII, p. 840.
8. Bispham, in *Century Magazine*, December, 1893, vol. XXV, p. 242.

NOTES

9. Lawrence Hutton, *Edwin Booth*, p. 3.
10. Royle, in *Harper's Magazine*, May, 1916, vol. cxxxii, p. 845.
11. To daughter, March 2, 1873, Grossmann, p. 36.
12. *Vagrant Memories*, p. 168.
13. Clara Morris, *Life on the Stage*, p. 162.
14. Aldrich to Taylor, October 9, 1866, in Ferris Greenslet, *The Life of Thomas Bailey Aldrich*, p. 83.
15. Bispham, in *Century*, December, 1893, vol. xxv, p. 243.
16. *Ibid.*, November, 1893, p. 132.
17. *Ibid.*, p. 133.
18. Grossmann, p. 3.
19. To Miss E. F. Cary, October 15, 1864, Grossmann, p. 166.
20. To Badeau, March 3, 1863, Grossmann, p. 141.
21. Horace Traubel, *Walt Whitman in Camden*, vol. i, p. 355.
22. *Ibid.*, vol. i, p. 456.
23. Malone, in *Forum*, July, 1893, vol. xv, p. 598.
24. Winter, *Life*, p. 111.
25. Charles Townsend Copeland, *Edwin Booth*, p. 102.
26. Winter, *Life*, p. 129.
27. To Cist, April 20, 1879, Shaw MS.
28. *Vagrant Memories*, p. 187.
29. Royle, in *Harper's Magazine*, May, 1916, vol. cxxxii, p. 849.
30. *Actors and Actresses of Great Britain and the United States*.
31. *Vagrant Memories*, p. 190.
32. To a young actor, August 9, 1866, Shaw MS.
33. Winter, *Life*, p. 141.
34. To daughter, May 30, 1875, Grossmann, p. 42.
35. Charles Townsend Copeland, *Edwin Booth*, p. 107.
36. To Winter, February 22, 1880, *Vagrant Memories*, p. 210.
37. Malone, in *Forum*, July, 1893, vol. xv, p. 601.
38. Royle, in *Harper's Magazine*, May, 1916, vol. cxxxii, p. 840.
39. Winter, *Life*, p. 107.
40. *Ibid.*
41. Winter, *Life*, p. 133.
42. To Ewer, December 19, 1880, Grossmann, p. 219.
43. To Major Walters, July 29, 1884, Shaw MS.
44. To daughter, March 16, 1891, Grossmann, p. 116.

NOTES

45. To daughter, February 27, 1876, Grossmann, p. 46.
46. To Miss Cary, January 10, 1865, Grossmann, p. 167.
47. To Winter, January 11, 1883, Winter, *Life*, p. 405.
48. *Vagrant Memories*, p. 196.
49. To Winter, January 11, 1883, Winter, *Life*, p. 405.
50. To Bispham, April 30, 1889, in *Century*, December, 1893, vol. xxv, p. 248.
51. To daughter, February 27, 1876, Grossmann, p. 46.
52. Mrs. Thomas Bailey Aldrich, *Crowding Memories*, p. 36.
53. Charles Townsend Copeland, *Edwin Booth*, p. 145.
54. *Actors and Actresses of Great Britain and the United States*, p. 100.
55. To Ewer, October 1, 1877, Grossmann, p. 188.
56. To daughter, May 30, 1875, Grossmann, p. 42.
57. Malone, in *Forum*, July, 1893, vol. xv, p. 602.
58. Mrs. Thomas Bailey Aldrich, *Crowding Memories*, p. 28.
59. *Vagrant Memories*, pp. 200, 202.
60. Royle, in *Harper's Magazine*, May, 1916, vol. cxxxii, p. 848.
61. *Other Days*, p. 182.
62. Grossmann, p. 10.
63. Ferris Greenslet, *The Life of Thomas Bailey Aldrich*, p. 3.
64. To Bispham, October 27, 1879, in *Century*, November, 1893, vol. xxv, p. 137.
65. To Bispham, March 3, 1887, in *Century*, December, 1893, vol. xxv, p. 245.
66. To daughter, April 23, 1876, Grossmann, p. 49.
67. To Badeau, March 3, 1863, Grossmann, p. 142.
68. Bispham, in *Century*, November, 1893, vol. xxv, p. 132.
69. To Badeau, May 18, 1863, Grossmann, p. 147.
70. To Mrs. R. F. Cary, December 20, 1865, Grossmann, p. 174.
71. *Vagrant Memories*, p. 215.
72. To Winter, April 23, 1886, Winter, *Life*, p. 436.
73. *Ibid.*
74. Winter, *Life*, p. 222.
75. Winter, *Life*, p. 22.
76. To a Baltimore lady, June 18, 1867, Shaw MS.
77. To daughter, January 5, 1888, Grossmann, p. 85.
78. Charles Townsend Copeland, *Edwin Booth*, p. 134.

NOTES

79. To daughter, January 5, 1888, Grossmann, p. 84.
80. To Winter, April 23, 1886, Winter, *Life*, p. 434.
81. *Ibid.*
82. *Ibid.*, p. 436.
83. Clara Morris, *Life on the Stage*, p. 104.
84. *As You Like It*, Act IV, Scene 1.
85. *As You Like It*, Act II, Scene 5.
86. Aldrich to Winter, June 12, 1893, Winter, *Life*, p. 242.

VI. FRANCIS JAMES CHILD

Child, Francis James, *The English and Scottish Popular Ballads*, five volumes.   *Ballads.*
Child, Francis James, *A Scholar's Letters to a Young Lady*, edited by M. A. DeWolfe Howe.   *Letters.*
Gummere, F. B., Article on Child, in *Atlantic Monthly*, March, 1909, vol. 103.   Gummere.

1. Gummere, p. 422.
2. *Life*, in *Ballads*, vol. I, p. xxix.
3. *Ibid.*
4. Gummere, p. 423.
5. To Lowell, MS.
6. To Lowell, MS.
7. To Lowell, MS.
8. *Letters*, p. 47.
9. Gummere, p. 421.
10. *Life*, in *Ballads*, vol. I, p. xxix.
11. *Ballads*, vol. I, p. 88.
12. Lowell to Norton, Feb. 18, 1877, *Letters of James Russell Lowell*, vol. II, p. 192.
13. *Ballads*, vol. I, p. 96.
14. *Ballads*, vol. I, p. 244.
15. *Ballads*, vol. I, p. 270.
16. *Ballads*, vol. I, p. 322.
17. To Lowell, MS.
18. Nathaniel Southgate Shaler, *Autobiography*, p. 418.

NOTES

19. Article in Boston *Transcript*, September 17, 1896.
20. Gummere, p. 425.
21. Gummere, p. 423.
22. Edward Simmons, *From Seven to Seventy*, p. 41.
23. *Life*, in *Ballads*, vol. I, p. xxxi.
24. Edward Simmons, *From Seven to Seventy*, p. 41.
25. *Letters*, p. 101.
26. *Life*, in *Ballads*, vol. I, p. xxxi.
27. *Ballads*, vol. III, p. 240.
28. *Letters, Introduction*, p. xi.
29. To Lowell, MS.
30. *Letters*, p. 128.
31. *Letters*, p. 74.
32. *Letters*, p. 57.
33. W. D. Howells, *Literary Friends and Acquaintance*, p. 252.
34. Lowell to Norton, February 18, 1877, *Letters of James Russell Lowell*, vol. II, p. 192.
35. *Letters of Charles Eliot Norton*, vol. II, p. 29.
36. To Lowell, MS.
37. *Letters, Introduction*, p. viii.
38. *Letters*, p. 48.
39. *Letters, Introduction*, p. vii.
40. *Letters*, p. 60.
41. To Lowell, MS.
42. To Lowell, MS.
43. *Letters*, p. 25.
44. *Letters*, p. 137.
45. *Letters*, p. 6.
46. To Lowell, MS.
47. *Letters*, p. 77.
48. *Letters*, p. 83.
49. Gummere, p. 425.
50. To Lowell, MS.
51. To Lowell, MS.
52. *Ballads*, vol. III, p. 95.
53. *Letters*, p. 30.
54. *Letters*, p. 52.

NOTES

55. *Letters*, p. 118.
56. *Letters*, p. 17.
57. *Letters*, p. 54.
58. *Letters*, p. 4.
59. *Letters*, p. 53.
60. Gummere, p. 424.
61. *Letters*, p. 99.
62. Frank Preston Stearns, *Cambridge Sketches*, p. 53.
63. *Letters*, p. 19.
64. *Letters*, p. 22.
65. *Letters*, p. 18.
66. *Letters*, p. 13.
67. *Letters*, p. 23.
68. *Letters*, p. 55.
69. *Faery Queene*, book II, canto XII, stanza 75.
70. Sonnet CIX.

VII. ASA GRAY

Gray, Asa, *Letters*, edited by Jane Loring Gray, two volumes.
Letters.
Gray, Asa, *In Memoriam*, Cambridge, University Press, 1888.
In Memoriam.
Jordan, David Starr, *Leading American Men of Science*.
Jordan.

1. *Critic*, February 11, 1888, new series, vol. IX, p. 63.
2. *Letters*, vol. I, p. 4.
3. *Letters*, vol. I, p. 7.
4. Dr. Rothrock, quoted by Dr. John M. Coulter, in Jordan, p. 222.
5. Dr. Mackenzie, *In Memoriam*, p. 27.
6. *In Memoriam*, p. 28.
7. *Letters*, vol. I, p. 107.
8. *Letters*, vol. II, p. 372.
9. *Letters*, vol. II, p. 705.
10. *Letters*, vol. II, p. 490.
11. To Engelmann, May 22, 1862, *Letters*, vol. II, p. 472.
12. To Engelmann, February 20, 1862, *Letters*, vol. II, p. 471.

13. To his mother, February 7, 1835, *Letters*, vol. I, p. 48.
14. *Letters*, vol. I, p. 9.
15. To Darwin, June 16, 1874, *Letters*, vol. II, p. 647.
16. *Letters*, vol. II, p. 436.
17. To Darwin, July 7, 1863, *Letters*, vol. II, p. 508.
18. Darwin to Gray, July 23, 1862, *More Letters of Charles Darwin*, vol. I, p. 202.
19. John M. Coulter, in Jordan, p. 228.
20. *Nature*, vol. XXXVII, p. 376.
21. In *Memorial of Asa Gray* (American Academy of Arts and Sciences), p. 12.
22. Obituary in Boston *Transcript*, January 31, 1888.
23. To Mrs. Torrey, March 18, 1843, *Letters*, vol. I, p. 302.
24. John M. Coulter, in Jordan, p. 223.
25. *Letters*, vol. II, p. 627.
26. Quoted by John M. Coulter, in Jordan, p. 230.
27. Darwin to Hooker, July 13, 1856, *More Letters of Charles Darwin*, vol. I, p. 95.
28. Asa Gray, *Scientific Papers*, vol. II, p. 254.
29. *Letters*, vol. II, p. 481.
30. *Letters*, vol. I, p. 295.
31. *Letters*, vol. I, p. 323.
32. *Letters*, vol. II, p. 606.
33. Nathaniel Southgate Shaler, *Autobiography*, p. 110.
34. John Marcou, *Life, Letters, and Works of Louis Agassiz*, vol. II, p. 108.
35. Lesley to his wife, January 3, 1866, in *Life and Letters of Peter and Susan Lesley*, by their daughter, Mary L. Ames, vol. I, p. 506.
36. *Letters*, vol. I, p. 324.
37. To Dana, November 7, 1857, *Letters*, vol. II, p. 431.
38. Review of Chapman's *The Flora of the Southern States*, in *Silliman's Magazine*, November, 1860, Series II, vol. XXX, p. 137.
39. Dr. John M. Coulter, in Jordan, p. 225.
40. In *Memorial of Asa Gray* (American Academy of Arts and Sciences), p. 14.
41. To Torrey, March 25, 1844, *Letters*, vol. I, p. 319.

NOTES

42. *Ibid.*
43. To Torrey, January 2, 1839, *Letters*, vol. I, p. 93.
44. *Biographical Memoir of Joseph Henry*, in *Annual Report* of the Board of Regents of the Smithsonian Institution, 1878, p. 157.
45. *Letters*, p. 323.
46. Dr. John M. Coulter, in Jordan, p. 220.
47. To Torrey, March 22, 1834, *Letters*, vol. I, p. 43.
48. To Mrs. Torrey, March 2, 1843, *Letters*, vol. I, p. 301.
49. To Engelmann, June 22, 1843, *Letters*, vol. I, p. 305.
50. To Mrs. Gray, 1847, *Letters*, vol. I, p. 350.
51. *The Letters of Charles Eliot Norton*, vol. II, p. 187.
52. *Letters*, vol. I, p. 324.
53. *Letters*, vol. I, p. 322.
54. Dr. Mackenzie, *In Memoriam*, p. 27.
55. To Charles Wright, January 17, 1848, *Letters*, vol. I, p. 353.
56. To W. J. Hooker, March 30, 1842, *Letters*, vol. I, p. 283.
57. To W. J. Hooker, May 20, 1841, *Letters*, vol. I, p. 279.
58. To Sir Edward Fry, November 10, 1883, *Letters*, vol. II, p. 747.
59. Dr. John M. Coulter, in Jordan, p. 222.
60. *Letters*, vol. II, p. 424.
61. *Letters*, vol. II, p. 430.
62. To G. F. Wright, September 15, 1875, *Letters*, vol. II, p. 657.
63. Asa Gray, *Natural Science and Religion*, p. 64.
64. *Life and Letters of Charles Darwin*, vol. II, p. 444.
65. *Ibid.*, vol. II, p. 67.
66. *Ibid.*, vol. II, p. 119.
67. Wyman MS., kindly communicated to me by Professor William M. Davis.
68. *Ibid.*
69. *More Letters of Charles Darwin*, vol. I, p. 10.
70. To his father, June 9, 1834, *Letters*, vol. I, p. 47.
71. *Letters*, vol. II, p. 682.
72. To W. M. Canby, October 28, 1878, *Letters*, vol. II, p. 683.

INDEX

INDEX

career, 89–91; his attitude on tariff, 90, 93, 122; effects of his late education, 91; his reading, 92; accustomed to solitary thought, 92; as Congressman, 93; his oratory, 93; as Secretary of War and Vice-President, 94; becomes sectional, 94, 95; as to his consistency, 94, 95; a supporter of nullification, 95; opposed to capitalism, 96; his attitude toward the Constitution and State Rights, 97–99, 123–27; his view of slavery, 97, 122, 123; his 'Disquisition on Government,' 98; his distrust of democracy, 99; his belief in minority representation, 99; his theory of 'concurrent majorities,' 99; his proposition for two consuls, 99; his insistence on the infallibility of reason, 100, 101, 118, 122; his self-confidence, 101; as man of business, 102; his 'autobiography,' 102, 106; his private concerns, 103; his plantation, 104; his slaves, 105, 114; extent of his interest in science and philosophic thought, 106, 107; his religion, 107, 111; depth of his thinking, 108, 109; his correspondence, 109; his emotional life, 109–11; his family life, 111, 112; his death, 113, 114; his diversions, 115; his ideals of friendship, 115, 116; his social efforts, 116; his social charm, 117; his conversation, 117, 118; his lack of humor, 118; his quarrels, 118, 119; and Jackson, 119; his ambition for the presidency, 120, 121; his speculation on finance, 122

Calhoun, Mrs. John C. (Floride Calhoun), 88, 91, 94

Candolle, Augustin Pyramus de, his 'Théorie Elémentaire,' 268

Capitalism, Calhoun's opposition to, 96

Carlyle, Thomas, quoted on Thackeray, 7

Centralization, in United States Government, 124–27

Channing, Edward, referred to, 22; on Calhoun's 'Disquisition on Government,' 98

Cheney, Mary Y. *See* Greeley, Mrs. Horace

Chestnut, Mary Boykin, anecdote of Calhoun told by, 108

Child, Francis James, chronology of his life, 204; his work on old English ballads, 205, 210; his persistence in work, 206–09; his lectures and readings, 209, 210; his gift of apt and delicate expression, 210, 211; his relations with colleagues, 212, 213; his relations with pupils, 213; variety of his interests, 215; his passion for justice, 216; his political activity, 216; his human kindness, 217, 218; his shyness, 218, 219; his humor, 218, 220, 221, 223; his charm, 220; his letters, 220–23; his richness of heart, 222; his reading, 223–25; his religious belief, 226, 227; his interest in Nature, 228; his appreciation of music, 229; his love of the old songs, 229–32; his contrast of work and song, 230; his love of roses, 232–36

Child, Mrs. Francis James, 204, 222

Cicero, compared with Webster, 15

Clay, Henry, chronology of his life, 44; compared with Webster and Calhoun, 45, 84, 85; his career, 45–47; his education, 47; no sign of æsthetic emotion in, 48; his immediate personal relations, 48, 49; his family, 49–51; his relations with his slaves, 52; his domestic finances, 52–54; as a lawyer, 54–56; his eloquence, 54–56, 69–71; his religion, 56, 57; his sociability, 57, 58; his hospitality, 58; as a talker, 58, 59; his humor, 59, 60; his social diversions, 60–62; his relish for cards, 61, 62; his friends, 62–64; his hostilities, 65, 66; his duels, 66; his popularity, 67, 68; his sensibility, 68; his capacity for work,

INDEX

71; his occupancy of the Speakership, 72; as leader of Whig Party, 72, 73; his ambition, 73–76; his political efforts, 76–81; called 'The Great Pacificator,' 78; his compromises, 78–81 (cf. 5, 27); his patriotism and sincerity, 81, 82; his democratic feeling, 82, 83; his belief in the Union, 83; his Americanism, 84; embodied the spirit of the West, 85; as to his consistency, 95; slavery hated by, 97; on Calhoun, 116

Clay, Mrs. Henry (Lavinia Hart), 44, 49, 50; the watchful assistance of, 53, 54; anecdote of, 62

Compromise, Missouri, 44, 46, 80; tariff, 44, 46, 81; slavery, 44, 47, 81, 91; Clay's view of, 78–81; in the Constitution, 79, 80, 98

'Concurrent majorities,' 99

Consistency, in action, 95

Constitution of United States, the highest type of political wisdom, 14; the grand example of compromise, 79, 80, 98; Patrick Henry's objections to, 125

Constitutional Convention, 127

Cooper libel suits, 162

Copeland, Charles Townsend, on Booth, 179, 183, 198

Curtis, George Ticknor, biographer of Webster, 37, 38

Cushman, Charlotte, 183

Dana, Charles Anderson, of *The New York Tribune*, 157

Dartmouth College case, 20

Darwin, Charles, 243, 245, 252; his candor and modesty, 239; quoted, 246, 266–68; his human attractiveness, 250; his willingness to recognize other points of view, 251; controversy over his theories, 253; his theories of Evolution, 265; and Gray, 265–67

Davis, Jefferson, 25, 97

Davis, Mrs. Jefferson (Varina Howell), on Calhoun, 89, 93, 117, 118

Democracy, distrust of, 99

Demosthenes, 15

Devlin, Mary. *See* Booth, Mrs. Edwin

Dwight, Timothy, his prediction with regard to Calhoun, 91

Dyer, Oliver, quoted on Clay, 63; on Calhoun, 117, 118

Eastman, Abigail. *See* Webster, Mrs. Ebenezer

Ellsworth, William Webster, on Booth, 172

Emerson, R. W., 39, 40; quoted on Webster, 12, 19, 20; his optimism, 110

Erwin, Mrs. (Ann Clay), 50

Eulogy of Jefferson and Adams, Webster's, 21

Evolution, Darwinian theories of, 265–67

'Federalist, The,' 92

Finance, Webster's study of, 23; Calhoun's speculation on, 122

Fletcher, Grace. *See* Webster, Mrs. Daniel

Foote, Samuel A., Senator, 25

Fort Hill, Calhoun's plantation, 104

Foster, Prof. Herbert Darling, in *The American Historical Review*, 27

Franklin, Benjamin, compared with Horace Greeley, 142

Fugitive Slave Law, 5, 27

Fuller, Margaret, on Horace Greeley, 145

Furness, Horace Howard, Booth's correspondence with, 181

Gallatin, Albert, on Clay, 74

Gautier, Théophile, 262, 263

Ghent, peace of, 44, 46, 61, 64

Girard College case, 20

Godkin, Edwin Lawrence, on Greeley and *The New York Tribune*, 158, 162

291

INDEX

Goethe, Wolfgang von, 51
Goodale, George L., on Gray, 247, 256
Goodridge case, 19
Gould, law teacher, 91
Gray, Asa, chronology of his life, 238; his writings and correspondence, 239, 240, 254, 255; his career, 240; his reading, 241; as a writer, 241; his religious feeling, 242; his feeling for beauty, 242, 243; his patriotism, 243, 244; his financial means, 244; his recreations, 245; his love of animals, 246; his cordiality, 246, 247; his scientific friendships, 247, 248; his patience, 248; as a teacher, 248, 249; influence of scientific spirit in, 250–52; his disposition to argumentation, 252–54; as a critic and reviewer, 254–56; his ambition, 257; his energy, 258; his ease and speed, 259; his thoroughness, 259, 260; his difficulties and drawbacks, 261, 262; his observation of natural facts, 262–64; his pursuit of the truth, 264, 265; his attitude toward Darwinian theories of Evolution, 265–67; his delight in growth of knowledge, 267–69
Gray, Mrs. Asa, 238, 246, 254, 261
Greek affairs, Webster's speech on, 21; Clay's attitude toward, 77
Greeley, Arthur, son of Horace Greeley, 130, 135
Greeley, Horace, chronology of his life, 130; his passion for work, 131–33, 140, 141; his nerves, 132; his boyhood and youth, 133, 138; his eccentricity of dress, 134, 135; his two interests, 137; his diversions, 138–40; his reading, 140; his thinking, 141; compared with Franklin, 142; his religion, 142–44; his personal benevolence, 144; his advice, 145; a born reformer, 146–48; his optimism, 148, 149, 161; in the Civil War, 149, 150; his participation in political activity, 150, 151; eager for public office, 151; his association

with Seward and Weed, 152; his Congressional career, 152; nominated for presidency, 153, 154; his ambition, 154, 155; his books, 154; as editor, 155–66; his ideal for a journalist, 161; his style of speech and writing, 162; his argumentativeness, 163
Greeley, Mrs. Horace, 130, 136, 137
Greenslet, Ferris, on Booth's letters, 192
Gummere, F. B., 213, 227, 231

Hale, Dr., 220
Hamlet, Booth identified with, 169, 199
Hart, Lavinia. See Clay, Mrs. Henry
Hartford Convention, 25
Hayne, Robert Young, Webster's reply to, 2, 5, 15, 25, 26
Henry, Joseph, 258
Henry, Patrick, his objections to the Constitution, 125
Hone, Philip, on Webster as an orator, 18
Hooker, Sir Joseph D., on Gray, 247
Hooker, Sir William J., 247
Howells, William D., 220; anecdote of, 186
Hülsemann, George, Webster's correspondence with, 23

Imagination, creations of, 169
Ingersoll, Charles Jared, Webster's attack on, 18, 31
Internal improvements, Clay's efforts for, 78; favored by Calhoun, 93
Irving, Sir Henry, 183

Jackson, Andrew, 5; his hostility to Clay, 65, 77; his hostility to Calhoun, 94, 119
James, Henry, 220
James, William, 220, 222
Janauschek, Fanny, 183
Jaques ('As You Like It'), 199, 200
Jefferson, Joseph, quoted on Booth's theater, 184

INDEX

Kean, Edmund, Booth's study of, 181, 194

Kinsman, Henry W., partner of Webster, 31

Kittredge, George L., on Child, 206, 209, 214, 216

Lamb, Charles, 148

Law, Webster's view of, 14; Clay's view of, 54

Lawyer, nurtured by tradition and precedent, 14

League of Nations, an objection to, 125

Le Clerc, Mlle., 230

LeRoy, Caroline. *See* Webster, Mrs. Daniel

Lesley, Peter, 253

Lincoln, Abraham, anecdote of Webster told by, 11; an American type, 39, 40; his eulogy of Clay, 69, 71, 83, 84; on Horace Greeley, 150

Lodge, Henry C., his 'Life of Webster,' 5, 27

Loring, Jane L. *See* Gray, Mrs. Asa

Lowell, James R., 42, 211; quoted, 207, 220; on Child's reading of Chaucer, 209, 210; verses of, on Gray, 250

McElrath, business manager of *The New York Tribune*, 157

McVicker, Mary F. *See* Booth, Mrs. Edwin

Malone, John, on Booth, 184

Marryat, Capt., guest of Clay, 60

Marshall, John, and Webster, 21; and Clay, 66

Martineau, Harriet, quoted on Clay, 58, 59; quoted on Calhoun, 89

Massachusetts Constitution, 41

Maury, Mrs. Sarah Mytton, 95; on Calhoun, 105, 114

Meigs, William M., biographer of Calhoun, 101, 106

Memphis Convention for development of Mississippi Valley, 93

Mendenhall, Quaker, 52

Mexican War, 90

Minority representation, 99

Missouri Compromise, 44, 46, 80

Modjeska, Helena, 183

Nast, Thomas, 153

New York Times, The, 158

New York Tribune, The, 150, 156–66

New Yorker, The, 131, 156

Newspaper, the, is anti-religious, 160; is anti-social, 160

Norton, Charles E., 220, 261

Nullifiers and Nullification, 5, 46, 81, 88, 90, 95, 99

Omar Khayyam, quoted, 189, 190

Parrington, Prof. Vernon Louis, *The Romantic Revival in America,* 13 *n.*

Players Club, 185

Plumer, William, on a conversation of Webster, 36

Plymouth Speech, Webster's, 2, 21

Providence Railroad *vs.* City of Boston, 20

Public lands, sale of, Clay's attitude toward, 77

Radicalism, Calhoun's, 96

Randolph, John, his quarrel with Webster, 9; his quarrel with Clay, 66, 67

Raymond, Henry Jarvis, of *The New York Tribune,* 157

Reason, as guide in human affairs, 100

Rhodes, James Ford, on Webster, 32; on Clay, 68

Ripley, Mrs., teacher of Child, 232

Roses, 232–36

Royle, Edwin Milton, on Booth, 171, 172

Sacco and Vanzetti, 126

Sainte-Beuve, Charles Augustin, favorite sentence of, 269

Salvini, Tommaso, 183

Scholar's life, 205

INDEX

ency, 95; on Calhoun, 115; Horace Greeley on, 154, 155
  Speeches: Bunker Hill Speeches, 21; Dartmouth College case, 20; Eulogy of Jefferson and Adams, 21; Girard College case, 20; Goodridge case, 19; Greek affairs, 21; Hayne, reply to, 5, 15, 25, 26; Ingersoll, attack on, 18, 31; Plymouth Speech, 2, 21; Providence Railroad *vs.* City of Boston, 20; Seventh of March Speech, 27, 37; White murder case, 19
Webster, Mrs. Daniel (Grace Fletcher), 2, 28
Webster, Mrs. Daniel (Caroline Le-Roy), 2, 28
Webster, Ebenezer, father of Daniel, 10, 28
Webster, Mrs. Ebenezer (Abigail Eastman), 10

Webster, Ezekiel, brother of Daniel, 10, 28
Weed, Thurlow, and Clay, 59; his association with Greeley and Seward, 152
Wendell, Barrett, his tribute to Child, 212
Whig Party, 72
White, Andrew D., quoted on Horace Greeley, 147
White murder case, 19
Whitman, Walt, on Booth, 177, 178
Winter, William, on Booth, 171, 173, 178–82, 188, 197
Wise, Henry A., on Clay, 75
Wyman, Jeffries, letter of Gray to, 266
Wythe, George, Chancellor, Clay protected by, 46